IN MY FATHERS HANDS

God's Grace. My Testimony.

RADICA QUACKENBOS

CROSSBOOKS
PUBLISHING

CrossBooks™
A Division of LifeWay
1663 Liberty Drive
Bloomington, IN 47403
www.crossbooks.com
Phone: 1-866-879-0502

Scripture taken from the King James Version of the Bible.

First published by CrossBooks 5/11/2011

ISBN: 978-1-6150-7845-5 (sc)
ISBN: 978-1-6150-7846-2 (dj)

Library of Congress Control Number: 2011927801

Printed in the United States of America

This book is printed on acid-free paper.

To my God, for his wonderful work in my life.
To my loving husband, whom I have from the Lord,
For his encouraging support in writing my story
And for his faithfulness to God and the work he has been called to do.
To my children and grandchildren, whom I love dearly, and for
whom I thank God daily.
To the many whose lives will be touched by my story.
To my friend Teri who helped edit the content.
To the precious woman I cared for.
To my Mother-in-law for encouragement, and the wonderful
husband she provided me.
Thanks to all of you!

CONTENTS

INTRODUCTION

This is the true story of my life. I was born in a Communist country, and grew up without any knowledge of God. Many events in my life should have driven me far from God. My life was filled with hate, as I faced one disaster after another. When I was forty-three, circumstances led me to a close and personal relationship with my Heavenly Father. As I look back over my life, I now see that God had me in His hands all through the difficult times. I see how He fed and clothed me after my mother and father abandoned me. God was shaping me, even back then, for His purpose in my life today.

My walk with God for the last ten years has revealed to me the true value of my life. As I share my story, I hope that you will see the final outcome, more than the sad childhood and young adult life I had. I hope you will see how, even without knowing God, He was always there for me.

I don't tell this story to condemn or to attribute anything negative to the people in my past. God has always had me in His hands, and so I praise Him, even when I knew Him not, He was always there. Without my knowledge, God's power, mercy, and grace for my life were leading me to glorify Him for His care and intimacy with me today. Surviving all I went through, I now know Him in the greatest way possible, both personally and intimately. He is my Savior, my Lord, and my close friend.

It is my hope and prayer that as you read my story *In My Fathers Hands*, you will be able to see God's hand in your past and come to understand how much He wants to be included in your future. If your life is broken, you will see how He can repair it. If your life is blessed, I pray that you will be encouraged to reach out to the many people around you who themselves have broken lives.

I now travel with my husband around the world and help in the ministry God has given to us, sharing my testimony as the Lord opens doors, and supporting my husband's call to minister from the Word of God. We have many open doors. We step into each one with boldness and confidence in our God's ability to equip us for each task and use my testimony to bring healing and restoration to those within the body of Christ, and to those who never enter a church but need help finding release from their past, just as I have.

CHAPTER 1

MY CHILDHOOD

My name is Radica Quackenbos. I was born October 03, 1957, in Yugoslavia, now known as Serbia. My mother and father were young teenagers. My mother got pregnant, and during her pregnancy she decided that she did not love my father any longer and made a decision to leave him right after my birth. When I was born, my mother brought me home from the hospital, packed her belongings, and moved out, leaving me with my father.

My father was an alcoholic and a gambler. He was young and he did not care for anyone but himself. He was gone most of the time, as most alcoholics are. I can't remember my father being around. I remember one time when I was three or four years old, I was walking the streets alone. A man found me and took me to the police station. No one there seemed to know who I was. They made a search of the town, called Veliki Popovic. It was a small town and no one in this town seemed to know who I belonged to. The police were circulating a picture of me in the markets and asking if anyone knew who I was. Soon an elderly lady, upon seeing my picture, told the police she knew my name was Radica. She said she knew my father; he was her neighbor. She took me home to my father's house from the police station, but my father was not there. They searched for him for about a week and found him trying to leave Yugoslavia and enter into the country of Austria. They arrested him and brought him back home.

I don't know or remember who cared for me that week, but I remember being in the police station quite some time. I was getting lollipops from the officer's, and they were showing me my picture in the paper. This made me feel special. A short time passed, and I remember my father got married to a woman whom he had just met at the bus station. *Marriage in Yugoslavia is simple: you simply bring a woman home to live with you.* He brought her home to be my baby sitter and left me alone with her, because the police were watching him. This way, it appeared to the police as if someone was watching me when he was gone. People thought he was married, and this arrangement made it appear that I was being cared for.

My father's new wife soon got pregnant. When she had the child, she packed up and left with the baby, leaving me with my father again. He still was spending his time drinking and gambling, as he always had done. He was about to lose the land which he had inherited from his father, my grandfather. My grandfather had died the day before my birth, so I never met him. I have no idea what he might have been like.

My grandmother, on my father's side, lived with my uncle, her first born child. She had given him her land and house in exchange for taking care of her until her death. They were not fond of my father; they hated his lifestyle, so we had no contact. Grandma would sneak over to see me from time to time, and she would often sneak me food.

The first and only Christmas I remember came when I was four or five. It was the day before Christmas and Grandma brought a single branch from a pine tree and placed it in a wine bottle, (the one item we had plenty of) and that branch became my Christmas tree. She placed a present next to the little tree. The present was a handmade purse. Grandma told me to open it the next morning. I was so excited because we did not have Christmas at my house. On Christmas morning, I discovered the purse was filled with walnuts, bread, and a few apples. On the bottom was a new pair of socks that Grandma had knitted just for me. This was my first and only Christmas present I received as a child. I was so excited to receive this gift. The walnuts became toys for me, as I could not crack them open. The most important thing in the bag was the pair of socks, made by my Grandma. They were like gold to me. I would cherish them more than anything I have received at any time in my life. As I remember, every other Christmas was spent alone at home.

The other holiday I remember was Easter. In our country people give eggs and food to strangers and leave food at gravesites. This is a Yugoslavian tradition. Another tradition is to leave food at the gravesite after a funeral, and every 40 days for a year. I would know when there was a funeral because they would pass by my house. We lived on the only road leading to the graveyard. I would then go to the gravesites and get as much food as I could, and run home so no one else would take it from me. I would sit on the stoop of our home and eat, always saving some for my daddy for when he would come home. I would have food for several days after Easter, as families would leave large amounts of their best foods at the gravesites. This is a custom of Yugoslavian's even today.

When I was just six years old, Grandma came to my house and asked me if I would like to go with her to find my mother. I asked Grandma what a mother was, for I had never had one. My only knowledge of motherhood came from watching the animals. I was so interested in the way a cow would nurse her calf, and lick it, and feed it. I would ask why the cow licked her calf, and Grandma would explain she was giving her baby a bath.

I was excited at the thought that my mother, whom I had not seen yet, would wash and feed me! This would be new to me, but I was excited that my mother would be there for me. Grandma said she knew someone who had knowledge of the town where my mother was living. This person said she thought my mother had gotten married to another man. I was so happy when Grandma washed my face, put clean clothes on me, and took me to my mother.

We would have an excessively long walk before the sun went down so we left home very early in the morning. It seemed to me as though we had walked forever. We walked through fields and areas I had never been before. In the late afternoon, we arrived at a house. This house was a much better place than the home where I lived with my father. My grandma called my mother's name from the gate a couple of times. "Rada, Rada," she called. You see, in my country, people put a fence or wall around their possessions to isolate themselves. Finally this woman came out, carrying a little baby girl in her arms. She opened the gate and recognizing my Grandma, she then kissed her on both cheeks. (*A greeting done by the people of Yugoslavia*). Oh, how I remember that day as she looked at me. Oh, how I wanted a kiss and a hug from her. I waited, but it did not come. She quickly invited my Grandma to come in. My Grandma was holding my hand very tightly, probably so I wouldn't run away, or maybe she just wasn't going to let go of me so easily. She introduced me to my mother. "This is your daughter Radica. Her father has gotten very bad with his drinking, and we don't know where he is. This child is left alone at the house, there's no one to care for her. You have to take care of her. You are her mother."

I was waiting for my mother to bend down, and hold and kiss me for the first time in my life. Instead all I heard was "Ah! She looks just like her father." My Grandma replied "No! Rada, she looks just like you. She has your face, your eyes; look at her, she looks just like you." My mother abruptly replied "absolutely not, she looks like her father." over and over I heard her repeat those words, "She looks just like her father."

I remember waiting to hear her say that I looked like my father, but that I was her child also. It never happened. So here I stood in front of my mother, who was a total stranger to me, and all she could say was, "Take her back, I'm not going to take care of her." "I have a daughter" (holding out the baby in her arms). "Look at her," she said, "Isn't she beautiful? She looks just like me. "Milanka," she kept saying, "look at her, see how beautiful she is." I responded, "Mommy, I look like you too. Grandma told me I look just like you." She then looked straight at me and said, "You are not my daughter, this is my daughter Milanka." She (meaning me) is her father's daughter," she told my Grandma. Grandma said, "We don't know where her father is, and someone has to care for her, and I am too old. I am losing my sight, I don't have a place of my own, and my son and daughter-in-law will not allow her to stay with me in their home. You have to take her, she's a girl and needs a parent, and she cannot live alone." My mother simply said, "That's not my problem, she is not my child, I'll have nothing to do with her." My Grandma said, "You gave birth to her, you cannot deny her?" Mother's response was, "I don't want to be reminded of the mistake I made, and this is my beautiful daughter Milanka." Grandma said to her, "Radica is also beautiful if you dress her and take care of her." Mother repeated, "I do not want to be reminded of the mistake I made." I remember thinking how could I be a mistake and why is she calling me a mistake. As my mother was speaking I was trembling with fear as I could see the anger on her face and hear it in her voice. I pleaded with Grandma not to leave me here with her, but she said I would be ok.

Grandma had given me instructions on the way. She said I was not to leave my mother's house regardless of what she might say to me. She said, "If you stay there, even outside, she will somehow, someday, have mercy on you since you are her daughter, and she will let you in and care for you as a mother should." As we were rejected, my Grandma gave me a big hug and a kiss. She whispered quietly to me, "Remember what I said, stay here and do not leave." "I love those freckles on your face!" she added. She always loved and told me about my freckles. I hated those freckles, but I learned to love them for Grandma's compliments about them. My Grandma then fixed my pony tail, turned and walked back out the gate and never looked back. I'm sure it must have hurt her as much as it hurt me. I stood there waving goodbye, but she did not look back, tears were flowing down my face as she left, and I called out, "Please don't leave me." I thought she might change her mind and come back before I lost sight of her.

I just stood there. I did not even know my mother, and as I stood there with a total stranger, being left here by the only person I thought loved me, I started crying to my own mother, "Take me home to my daddy." It was late, and it was now getting dark. I had walked all day with Grandma, and here I stood, outside my mother's house, being ignored as if I did not exist. I could see thru the window that my mother was taking care of the baby (my half sister). I saw her giving the baby a bath and feeding her, and then she and the baby went to bed, without recognizing me in any way. All this time I was watching from the front porch step, and my six year old heart was breaking as I wanted so much for her to hold me in her arms and say I will take care of you. I love you. Or, don't be afraid. Those words would have meant so much to me, but I never heard them.

I waited a short time before I called out, "Mommy! Where will I sleep?" She responded, "Sleep where you slept before." I said, "But I sleep at daddy's house. I don't know how to go there. Grandma said to stay here, and not to leave, because you will love me, for I'm your daughter." But she just ignored me. She made believe she was sleeping in her bed. She turned towards her baby in a hugging position, and she pretended to be asleep. I waited and waited, and soon, I ventured into the house. I crawled into the bed behind her, my half sister on the one side of her and me behind her on the other. I felt so safe with my hand touching my mommy. I had always had to sleep by myself, often crying myself to sleep, wondering if my daddy would come home. I usually fell asleep like that, crying, wondering, and alone. But not on this night! Not at this moment. I was safe. I was with my mommy.

In the morning, mommy got up and took care of the baby and made breakfast. I went outside, fascinated that she had so many animals. I had seen our neighbors with animals, but daddy and I had never had any of our own. I remember mommy had a lot of animals. I fed the chickens and ducks that morning, and I remember I told the chickens how great it was to sleep with my mommy last night. I told them my daddy was coming for me. I also cleaned the alley where the ducks had made a mess. I was hoping mommy would love me for helping to clean things up. Grandma had told me to be a good girl and help clean the house for mommy, and help mommy so she would love me.

Maybe I was trying to earn her love somehow, in some way. I entered the house hoping for food and love. She was already eating so I told her what I had done. She, replied, "I didn't tell you to do that." She then left the table, so I ate what was left over from their breakfast. It wasn't much, but I was hungry. That day as she was working in the house with the baby, I tried to play with my sister. My mother told me not to touch her. Oh, how I wanted to be that little girl, and how I wanted that love. I could see my mother truly loved my sister, but why not me? "Go back to your father," she said. I told her, "I don't know how." She responded: "The same way you came." I asked my mom to get my daddy for me, so he could take me home. She just acted as if she did not hear me. I told her, "I have a bed at his home," and asked her to take me there. She just ignored me.

I remember going outside and playing with the animals all day. At evening she told me to stay out of her house. "Go home, go home," she said over and over, "go to your father's house." I remember she locked the door that evening and went to bed with her daughter. I could see thru the window she was in bed and the lights were out. In my fear I cried out to mommy to please open the door; I wanted my daddy I was scared of the dark. She was not listening to me. I now started pleading for Grandma. I asked her to please get them for me, I wanted to go home. I walked around for some time; then went to the barn. I put some hay into the feed trough and slept there for the night. I cried so much. These cows and horses are so big, I thought, it's cold, and I'm alone and scared to death. Where is my daddy? I thought, "Will he come for me?"

The next morning I told my mother where I had slept, but it was as if she never heard me. I knew she did hear me, but she did not care. I cried and cried. She would tell me to do the chores, and no matter what I would do it was not good enough. A few weeks passed, and I stuck around like a stray cat, I would sneak food from the house, but now looking back, I think maybe she left it out so I could find it.

After a few weeks, her husband, who worked in Switzerland, came home. I heard her tell him the story of how Grandma brought me there. He told her she must accept me and let me live there, but she refused. I was so dirty. My hair was filled with lice from the barn, so my stepfather gave me a bath, and washed my hair. I smelled so good. This was my first bath with soap that I could remember. He also gave me some food, and praised me, saying how pretty I was. I never had anyone praise me before except for Grandma, who had brought me here; so I was really enjoying this. I thought I might be accepted because he seemed to accept me.

The next day he bought me some clothes, shoes, a book to read, and a bag with pencils. I was so happy for the first time I had **new** clothes and **new** shoes. I asked him if he knew where my daddy was and if he could take me home. His answer was this was my home now. After a conversation with him about how my mother treated me and rejected me, he brought me into the kitchen and showed me a bed, sitting right there in the kitchen. He said, "This is your bed. You're a big girl and you shall sleep here by yourself." He asked where I had been sleeping and I told my stepfather I was sleeping with my friends (meaning the animals). He then explained they were not friends, but animals. As I lay there that night I called out to my daddy to hurry and come for me. I would tell him in my sobs where I was and ask him to hurry. I thought he might hear me and come for me. My mother and stepfather fought over that, and I could hear them argue.

When my stepfather returned to work about a month later, my mother started abusing me. She would hit me and kick me, telling me to go home. "You are just like your father," she would say. She would hit me with a rolling pin on my head and on my arms. I still have a mark on my wrist today from it. She would send me to take care of her sheep throughout the day but without water or food. Sometimes I would come home soaked from rain, or filthy from dirty paths, she seemed to care less.

She would hit me, while being out of control, often stepping on me. Whatever she could grab with her hand, would be used to beat me. I remember one day she was arguing with somebody else, and her anger was to be taken out on me later. She said she would teach me a lesson, but how was I to learn a lesson from somebody else's mistake. While beating me, she would say, "You're just like your father." I wonder if when she looked at me, if she was really seeing him. Maybe she was beating him up through me. I remember I was bleeding from my ear and my nose after being beaten with a rolling pin. After my mother had finished beating me, she turned and walked away while I lay on the floor in the blood, ignoring the pain. The blood was coming out of my nose and ear. (I still have a scar on my head from that beating). As I lay there, I thought my mommy will come back and take care of me. She's beaten me. I'm lying on the ground, I'm bleeding, and my mother just went into the house as if nothing happened. I remember thinking, does she ever cry for what she's done? There would be no response. I had been badly beaten, and it was painful, but the pain of realizing that my mother could care less about me was far greater than the physical pain in my body. Until this day I still wonder if my mother felt any pain in her heart for what I was going through. How could anybody be so heartless? To this day, my mother is as cold-hearted as she was back then, caring for nobody but herself and how she can use others for her own advantage. I could not understand how my sister was treated with loving care, never abused, provided for, and obviously loved, and I was treated worse than an animal.

As the days would go by I would wonder how anyone could bring me to this woman, called my mother. In my heart, I tried to deny that she was my mother, but as I looked at her I saw that I looked just like her. One day when my mother was in a good mood, I asked her, "Why don't you like me? What have I done to make you treat me like this?" She responded, "I don't like you, and I can't raise you." I asked her, Why not? You're rich, you obviously have a place for me to sleep, but you don't let me sleep in the house, why?" She simply said, "I can't, I told you to go back to your father." I asked my mother, "You beat me, why don't you do me a favor and just kill me? You don't want me, they don't want me, and nobody cares for me." She responded, "Your father cares for you, go back to him." I told my mother, "Daddy loves me and I love him, but he leaves me there in the house by myself." I told her, "My daddy never hit me." Her response was, Well good for you. Go to him."

I thought if I told my mother that my father did not hit me things would change. I thought she would stop hitting me. I thought if I told her my father loved me, maybe she would be jealous and start loving me, because jealousy ruled her life. As a child I obviously did not know that this jealousy would just make her abuse me more, because I reminded her of my father and that would make her despise me even more.

She reminded me as a little child that I would always be poor, just like my father and nobody would want me. Oh, she was so wrong, but I would not find this out for many years. I told my mother that day, "I will never be poor, for my father will provide for me." This day I realized as a child that to speak good about my father would make my mother angry, so I would often talk about my father. I would talk about his love for me, knowing it would make her angry. I was going to get beat either way, so this way I tried to hurt her back by reminding her that my daddy loved me and she didn't.

One day as a small child six years old, I was looking up in the sky and I saw a plane flying overhead as I was tending the sheep. Not knowing what an airplane really was, I said out loud, "Someday I will fly on that plane, far, far from here. I will have nice clothes and good food. I will never come back to this place." I went home and told my mother. She laughed in my face, telling me I had a great imagination. Forty-five years later my mother would tell me this story, when she saw it had come to pass. She said to me, "Everything you spoke as a child came to pass in your life. How?" she wanted to know.

One day as I was taking the sheep to the field I came up with an idea how I might get her to show some compassion on me. I spotted a bee hive. I went and disturbed them causing them to sting me. I caught some of them, and placed them on my face, very close to my eyes, letting them sting me. As my face swelled I ran home screaming, "Mommy, mommy, look what happened to me." In my mind I could see my mommy running out to take care of me, having compassion on me, asking me what happened, and taking care of me. I had no idea all the stingers would swell my face, or of the pain they would cause especially around my eyes. I was so desperate for somebody to just love me and care what happened. I ignored the pain and I would have gladly suffered it just to have a hug from my mother, to hear her say, what happened to you, as if she cared.

I was expecting her to hug and care for me, feeling sorry for my condition. She looked at me and said, "Look at you. You look like a devil. You look disgusting." She simply spit on the ground in front of me and went back in the house. I felt worse pain from being rejected than I did from the bee stings. My plan had failed, if she had only asked me if I was ok, I would have felt better, but there I stood rejected again and covered with painful bee stings. I went into the barn and told the cow how I felt. As I was pulling the stingers out of my face I realized this might not have been a good plan. I did not know that you had to remove the stingers after they stung you, and this was hurting and of course very unpleasant. I remember thinking, I don't know which hurts me more, the stings or the fact that my mommy does not care about me. As a child I was confused and looking for love and attention. I loved the cow as if she was my mother. As I would stroke its head and talk, I would tell the cow, "I'll be ok." It seemed like the cow understood me. I fell asleep in front of the cow with her licking my face, and did not wake up until the next morning.

Days, weeks, even months went by. I waited for my mother to accept me, but she did not accept me. I couldn't understand why. I told myself, my grandmother was wrong; my mother would not care for me no matter what I did. Winter was coming and I had only a few clothes, just what I was wearing. I could not understand why mommy did not dress me, wash me, or brush my hair like she did with her other child.

One night I was so cold I walked around trying to keep warm. I ended up at the sheep pen. They were sleeping, so I stood there looking at them, wondering and amazed at how the mother animals were taking care of their babies. I stood there, freezing, just staring at the sheep. One of them had two lambs, and she was taking care of both of them. I wondered how this sheep could have two babies, and love them both, but my mommy could not. One of these sheep stood up and came to me at the gate. She was making a noise, baa, baa. Somehow I knew she was calling me to come in her pen, and then a second sheep got up, making the same noise. They seemed to be looking right at me. One sheep started making a weird noise, it seemed to me as if the sheep was telling me to come lay down. Maybe it was just me, but I did, I lay down with the sheep. I curled up to the back of one of the sheep, (just like the night I crawled into mom's bed) and one of the other sheep came over and laid next to me. Now I had one on each side. It was so cold, but they kept me warm all that night. I felt so comfortable. I knew that these sheep had taken care of me. I remember how it seemed to me this sheep cared enough to see me cry, and in her way she seemed to be showing me with her head, come lay down. I will never forget how I felt that night; I had a safe place to go and lay down. I had the feeling that something cares for me and loves me. Unfortunately it was a sheep rather than my mother. I thought if these sheep were only my parents I would be loved. I fell in love with the sheep. To this day I cannot pass up sheep without feeling drawn to them. Even in other countries while traveling, I seek out fields where there are sheep.

I was the shepherd girl. It was my responsibility to take the sheep out to where the good grass grows each day, but at night, they were my safe place to sleep. I slept every night with the sheep. In the summer we would sleep outside under a roof cover, but when it is winter I would have to go into the barn because I couldn't stay out in the cold like the sheep can. In the barn I would sleep with the cows. It was snowing outside and of course, you couldn't go out in the snow. You couldn't take the sheep to the field in the winter, for there is no grass, and they stay inside during the winter. Each day I would feed them and talk to them, playing with them, they would lick my face. It seemed to me they were as happy to see me as I was to see them. In my heart I felt as if they really cared for me.

While staying in the barn, I developed cysts or some kind of sores all over my body. When my mother discovered them I thought she would care. I knew if the cow had gotten the sores she would take care of the cow, but she did not care that I had these sores. For several months, these sores would kind of heal up and then come back again.

Spring came and I began taking the sheep to the fields again. Another woman with her sheep began a conversation with me. She asked me about the sores, because they were on my face and could not be hidden. She asked if I had told my mother. I did not answer, but I started to cry. She asked if she could take care of them for me. She then went home, and when she returned she brought some black cream and rubbed it all over me. It relieved the pain. I think I was more comforted by the fact that somebody actually cared enough to take care of the sores than I was for having the medicine. I had these sores for several months and nobody cared, and yet this lady would come back every couple of days with her sheep and she would take care of the sores and bring me food. I have a permanent image in my mind of this lady, to this day I can see her face, feel her compassion, and hear her words. Forty some years later, I would encounter this lady, and recall the events of those days.

My mother would come home and punish me with a beating, or I would get slapped if anyone simply said good morning to me, or if anyone would speak nice about me. I had more than enough beatings as a child. One day at the very moment I was being beaten badly and my mother was talking to me like I was a dog, a woman walked in. This woman witnessed my mother beating me with a rolling pin over my head and on my face. The woman took the rolling pin from my mother, and began yelling at her. I remember her words to this day. She said, "What are you doing to this child?" My mother answered, "I will teach her a lesson. I told her to go away, and she keeps hanging around here." The woman said, "She is your daughter, she cannot go away; and where would she go? You have to accept her, she is your child." My mother got furious, saying, "She can go to be with her father, where she belongs." Later I found out this stranger was actually my mother's sister. She had compassion on me, she washed me, brushed my hair, and she even cried with me that day.

On that day, at the age of 7, I reached a decision, I would run away to avoid the beatings and being treated like this. My mother had more love for the pet dog than for her own flesh. I would see her feed and care for the dog while not caring for me at all. I was hurting inside so much, as a child would, not having anyone, especially their mommy, care about them. I decided it would be better for me at my daddy's house, but I did not know how to get there.

I asked an aunt where my daddy lived. She told me, but asked me, "You're not planning to go there, are you?" I responded, "No," but I started to remember some of the way back to daddy's home. I made a decision to run away from my mother's house when I was 7 years old. I thought my mother would come looking for me, but I would still go. I did. I ran away, and that day I made it all the way back to daddy's home.

When I arrived, my father was not home, the house was cold, and there was no food. We had a wood stove, one bed, a table, and two chairs. Nothing else. I didn't care about furniture, I cared about my daddy. I was waiting for daddy to come home. I spent my time looking through the window, waiting, imagining my daddy would come home, love me, and he would make everything better.

When anyone was seen walking down the road my direction, I would get all excited and say, "Daddy's coming." I would look through the window, but it was not daddy. Somebody else was just passing by. I cried and cried and called out my father's name loudly, "Daddy, come home, I'm here waiting for you." Days passed, and daddy did not show up.

The lady who lived next door to my daddy noticed that I was home. She questioned me about what had happened. "What are you doing here?" she asked. So I told her my daddy had come and brought me home. I was lying of course. She asked; "Where is your daddy now?" I lied again, telling her he went out, but he would be right back. She asked if I was hungry. It had been several days that I had gone without food, plus it had been a long walk home. I said, "Yes, I am hungry. As a matter-of-fact I haven't eaten today. My daddy has gone to buy food," I told her. She knew I was not telling the truth so she went home and brought me some food. I remember she came over with bread, it was stale, and some cheese, but oh, it tasted so good!

A few days later my grandmother found out that I had come back. She came to the house and asked what happened, I told her, "Grandma you made a mistake. That woman is not my mother, she doesn't even want me." I then told her about the sheep caring for their young. Grandma had an answer for everything, but I did not want to hear her anymore. "Just find my daddy," I said. Then I told her the whole story. I could take it no more. I had been abused. "That woman is trying to kill me," I said. "She doesn't love me. She keeps saying you are your father's daughter, go back home." I told my Grandma, "I don't know where daddy is, but I am bound to wait for him, he'll come back to love me."

One day I decided the way to get my daddy to return home was to cook dinner for him, and where ever he was he would smell the food and come home to eat. I took a couple of beans I found in the shed, I put them in a pot. They were dirty but I didn't know better. I added a little water, and I put them on the stove. Our stove was an old wood burning type. I tried to get some wood to start the stove, but I couldn't find any. Since there was no wood I decided to use an old pair of rubber shoes and a few old inner tubes from my dad's bicycle. I remember they were made of rubber, so I took a match with some paper and I started the fire. Before I knew it, the fire was so big it was coming out of the right side of the stove. This was not supposed to happen. I had seen daddy, and others, light the stove. I remember when the fire took off it got so big so very fast. I was screaming in terror. I don't know what exactly happened, but it was as if *someone just reached in* there and lowered the fire to a small flame. My terror was over. I looked into the pan to see if the beans were done, then I went back to the window, stood on the bed, looking out for daddy to come. I thought he would follow the smell of the beans, but he never showed up. I guess I fell asleep on the bed.

The next day I was awakened, when I heard footsteps inside the house. I thought that it would probably be my grandmother, coming back to check on me. It was my daddy! I thought, my daddy, my daddy is home. He asked me, "What happened with you, and what are you doing here?" I told him, "Daddy I have to be with you. My mother doesn't want me; she said I am your daughter and not hers. She's been hitting me and I couldn't take it anymore. Please daddy, please believe me." He promised he wouldn't take me back to mommy's home.

Daddy then went out, got some food and brought it home. I was so happy. I knew my daddy would come home. I told my daddy that I kept telling myself that he would come home, and "he did." I thanked my daddy many times that day for coming home to me. That night my father and I talked, and played on his bicycle for a very long time. As we rode around, he would kiss me on the head. We rode all the way to the bakery, where he bought me some fresh hot bread. He kept calling me; "My boy." I could smell the alcohol on his breath. I would correct him, but he kept calling me, "My boy." I guess I discovered that night my father wanted a boy, not a girl. But none the less I was here and he loved me. To this day I miss my daddy more than words can say.

I was with my daddy for about a month when the courts got involved. At this time they awarded me to my father and now he was going to be forced to take me to school and care for me. My father told the courts that I had been living with my mother, and she was very wealthy and would be able to provide better care for me than he could. The courts agreed that for me to go back to her would be best. My father explained this to me. My father told the courts he was going to get a job, set up a place for me and then take me back to be with him. After hearing this, I asked, "Don't you love me, Daddy?" My daddy was crying and hugging me as he said, "Yes I do, but you will have food and shelter there." I asked my father, "Why don't you understand? She abuses me, she treats me badly, and she makes me sleep in the barn." I tried to explain this to my father. "I want to be here with you, and I don't want to be over there," I said. My father said to me, "No, you will see, she will be nice to you after a while, she will love you." I wanted so badly to run away right then so I wouldn't have to hear this.

My daddy did not understand what I had gone through at my mother's house. I thought he just doesn't care or doesn't believe me. My daddy would try to explain to me that he was a poor man and could not take care of me. I did not care that my daddy was poor. I just wanted my daddy. I wanted him to change his mind and keep me. I told my daddy that day, "I don't need you to give me food." By this time I had learned how to get food. I've been okay without food, just getting what I could. I had lived on berries, apples, and prunes, and I had to steal them some of the time. I knew that I could take care of getting food for myself. I remember telling my father, "If you let me stay with you, I will get enough food for both of us. Just keep me here. I want to stay with you. I know how to get food."

My only concern was to stay with my daddy. I pleaded with daddy over and over that day. We were both crying so my father assured me, "One day I will come and get you and I will bring you back home." This was my daddy's promise, and it made me feel better. I asked my father, "Why does my mother not like you?" I added, "Why doesn't she like me, and why does she keep telling me I look like you, daddy?" My father responded, "You are *my* Daughter." I remember he kissed me, saying, "I know why she doesn't love me, I can tell you I promised her many things before she became pregnant with you, and I did not keep my promises because of the alcohol. It came between her and me, he hesitated a moment then said, "Maybe she is taking that anger out on you, I just don't know." He told me, "You will be okay. You look like her and you're going to be all right, she will love you one day. You are a nice kid. Any mother should be happy to have you, and she will change." He kept trying to assure me. In my heart I knew this was not true, but my father just did not understand.

My words seemed to mean nothing. Maybe he didn't believe it, or maybe he just wanted to be free to go back to his alcohol and gambling without responsibility. At least if I was at my mother's he would not be going to jail for not taking care of me. I even promised my dad, "If you just keep me, I will go to the bars with you. That way you can watch me in the bar and I will be with you. You will not have to miss me, I will be there with you in the bar and I will not miss you," I told him. I assumed that my father was missing me like I was missing him.

My father told me he was going to go look for job, and buy me a pretty dress and pretty shoes, but that never happened. This was my father's way of letting me go, and maybe, in his heart, believing he was doing the right thing. I did not believe he would do this. In my little childish heart I knew my daddy was trying to make me happy. He did not understand my only happiness was to have him close by, only him. At this point in my life the only thing that made me happy was being with my daddy. I could have cared less if he had any money, or any food, or anything. I just wanted daddy.

I began begging my daddy not to leave me. "I'm sorry, I'm sorry but I have to," my daddy said! He was crying. I felt like my daddy was leaving me like a stray puppy. "Go, don't worry," he said, "You're going to be okay." I said, "When you're not around I miss you and it makes me sad." My father hugged me and kissed me so many times. I kept asking daddy, "Are you coming back? Will you come for me, if I call?" He said he would. I said," please come for me soon daddy, I will wait for you like always. I waited a few days at my father's house, waiting for him to take me back to mother's house.

It was not long after this when my daddy put me on his bicycle, and we rode to Mama's house. It was several hours and along the way, I kept hugging my father's neck, kissing his neck, and telling him how much I loved him. I was hoping he would change his mind and turn around. I could see my father was crying, and his tears were dropping on my head. I can almost feel the bicycle bar today, but then I didn't care for I was close to daddy. I kept asking him, "Do you promise to come back, do you promise to come back?" He responded, "Yes," but I was still hoping my daddy would change his mind, turn around, and keep me with him.

We arrived near my mother's house. I could see my mother's house in the distance. There were many trees and my daddy was going to leave me there by the trees so I could go back to my mother's home. I asked my daddy if he could at least talk to my mother. "Could you go in the house and talk to her?" I said. "Could you tell my mother what you told me about her loving and taking care of me?" He responded, "I can't do that; she doesn't talk to me anymore."

My father then placed his hand inside of his jacket, and pulled out some candy, giving it to me. I remember a chocolate candy bar and some other type of candy. I especially remember the chocolate candy bar. My father had never bought me or gave me candy before this. This was the first time that my father had given me sweets. He said to me, "This is for you; don't forget me." He said, "You are so pretty, and you deserve the best. I love you, my freckle face; remember I love you, my sunshine." My father and I hugged and we cried together for what seemed like forever. I remember I grabbed him so tightly. To this day I can feel that closeness and that last hug from my father. My heart was so broken.

My father then took his bicycle, turned around, and started riding away. I began running after my father crying and screaming, "Daddy, come back; Daddy come back." I was chasing after him as fast as I could run. My daddy never looked back. He just took off riding as fast as he could peddle. It was not very long before he outran me. Upon losing sight of my father as he peddled over the top of the hill, I threw myself on the ground. I kept crying and calling my daddy, remembering that on the way he told me, *if you call me I will come back.*

I was scared and mad that he left. I didn't know what my mother was going to do now. I picked up the candies that my father had given me, for I had thrown them under the tree to run after him. I was standing by the tree, and I was kissing the chocolate candy bar. I remember to this day, I felt connected to my daddy just kissing the chocolate candy bar. It was the last thing daddy gave me. I stood there for a long time, candy bar in my hand, crying, kissing it, thinking that my daddy will turn around. He would come back, and surely he had to feel just like I felt.

I don't know how long it was, but finally I turned around, looking at the house where I would have to go, mommy's house. I was fearful of what might happen. I was sure I was going to get a beating, so I waited until dark to go home. I did not go to the house, instead I went to the barn to the sheep and cows, and it would be morning before I would let my mother know I was there. I remember telling the sheep, "I'm sorry I left you, but I'm back, and my daddy is going to build me a big house and I'm going to go and live with him and be very happy. But don't worry," I told the sheep, "you can come with me because my daddy is building a big house, you will have a place to stay with me the same way I have stayed in your house. We will always be together like we are now." Remember, I was a child and for me the sheep were my family. I believed my father was going to do this as any child would trust their daddy.

I ate that candy bar one day and then I took that wrapper from the candy bar, folded it up ever so carefully and placed it in my pocket. I carried that wrapper around for a long time; it was my only connection to my daddy. My pocket had holes and that wrapper would fall out from time to time, but I would somehow always find it. I decided it was better to bury it under a rock in the barn than to lose my connection with my daddy. Sometimes I would take it to school. When I would see other students enjoying chocolate in front of me, I would pull out my wrapper, telling with great joy how my daddy gave it to me. They would laugh at me and make fun of me, but I did not care. I would say, "My daddy loves me. He bought me a candy bar." Oh, I would brag about that paper. I would tell them my daddy was coming back sometime and how he was going to build me a big house and take me home with him. I was sure their fathers had given them candy as mine had given me, so I would brag about my daddy. I don't remember what finally happened to it. I guess it just got lost over the long period of time that I had it.

Someone called the police on my mother, I think it might have been my father. They reported her abusing me. She was told; she had to enroll me in school. So here I was going to school. My clothes were old, and I had no lunch and no books. All the other kids had their books and nice clothing, and I had worn out clothes, shoes, and was often unwashed. I was only sent to school to keep her from getting into trouble with the school.

It was hard looking at the other kids all washed, and my clothes filthy. I looked awful and it hurt me, wounding my spirit inside. I was crushed because the kids in my school would not even play with me. I had no friends; it seemed to me as if they wanted me to just go away. I started being abusive to other children. I would hit and beat them. I thought if I took out my anger on the smaller ones, I would show I was tough and maybe they would be afraid to pick on me. I would even pick on my smaller half-sister, as I saw my mother play and care for her and it made me angry. She would buy her nice clothes, new shoes, even jewelry. My mother's rejection of me was not because she could not afford me, but a choice she made because she hated my father. I began to hate myself at this time, believing I was somehow different, unlovable, not worth anything.

I decided one day, if I just killed my half-sister, maybe mommy would love me in her place. I would privately beat her up. She would run to mommy screaming for protection and I remember my mother asking me, "What are you trying to do?" I said, "I want to kill her, then you can have only me and love me the way you love her." I got a beating that day like never before. I realized I could not kill her actually, for my sister, when she looked in my eyes, I could see she loved me. I would find out later my sister was having trouble understanding why our mother was totally different to each of us.

Someone at the school was getting the school supplies I needed, probably the teacher. I got into trouble beating up a boy in class one day, and the teacher sent a note home to my mother. I gave it to her, and she said she did not want to go to the school for me, and would not. So I told the teacher she was sick and could not come now, but would come next week. The teacher decided to pay my mother a visit at home. My teacher came to our home. That was not good for me. She was telling my mother, that she was not happy with the way I came to school, all dirty, my hair never brushed and I had lice. She said she was worried about the other children in the classroom. She told her to keep me home for a week, to get rid of the lice. She gave instructions to my mother on how to care for my hair, but she ignored the whole conversation.

As far back as I can remember my mother's main concern was having more possessions than anyone else in our town. It just seemed to drive her. I decided to run away again, but I wasn't going home to daddy this time. I decided I would go far enough to hide, but still close enough to see what would happen. I remember stealing people's laundry off their lines because I had no clothes. I would hide in the woods so no one could see me. I was so ashamed that I was dirty, often hungry, with little or no clothes except what I stole. I stole a dress and underwear from the teacher's clothesline one day, not even thinking she might recognize her own clothes. I wore them to school the very next day. I'm sure she knew they were hers but all she ever said to me was, "Radica that is a very nice dress." I thanked her and took my seat in the class room.

I would be taken back to my mother's house many times, and I would run away to keep the abuse from happening. I would try to fit in with the other children, but the anger inside me would quickly separate me from them, and it wouldn't take long for me to start fights. Each time I would fight I felt as if I was repaying my mother for the things she did to me. As I picked on others, in my mind I could see my mother beating me. I also thought if my father heard of the fights he would come and take me home. As well as I can remember, my childhood was a dark, lonely time with one disappointment after another.

Rejection was a lifestyle for me and I was unable to believe anyone could love a child who was rejected and despised by her own family. I would see some of my aunts from time to time, and have some food and a little playtime with their kids. This was usually not more than a day or so. They had their own children, so they would return me to my mother's house and leave me there. Sometimes I would at least get a bath and maybe some clothes from their kids. They were always used clothes, but they were clean. The clothes were good as new to me.

CHAPTER 2

TEEN YEARS

My mother had a sister and brother. I asked them if I could stay with them, but the answer was No! They had not built any relationship with my mother. They said my mother did not seek to have any relationship with her family, and my mother thought she was better than all the rest of them. I also met my grandfather on my mother's side. I asked him if I could live with him. My grandfather talked to my mother about it, and she convinced him not to let me. That was the last time I saw my grandfather. My Grandma on my mother's side had passed away when my mother was only fourteen, so I never met her.

By age eleven I started sleeping in the woods behind my mother's house. When she would go out, I would enter the house and steal food to eat. I wondered if she knew the food was missing. I would see my mother doing work around the house and I would just stay hidden. I started to go farther and farther from the house. I was sleeping in a valley, not too far away. It had a small creek running through it. Here I could wash in the creek and also drink the water. I would sleep close by the creek. It made me feel comfortable to have a supply of water. I also found a good supply of berries there, often satisfying myself by eating the berries.

One autumn evening I was near the stream and I heard a snake crawling in the dry crackling leaves and grass. I was scared to death and started crying out to make it go away. When I stopped crying, the noise was gone. I remember thinking, why does my mother not disappear like that when I cry? Why couldn't she be like the snake and just disappear? I would spend lots of time in the valley and often shepherds would pass there with their sheep. I would stare at the shepherds with a sad face and they would often give me some food, which helped because I was hungry most of the time. Some of them would question me about what I was doing there alone. I would tell them, that I was just on my way home. I was too young to think they might not believe me as they often passed there.

I would take the food they offered and pretend to be on my way to the city. Often I went to the bus station at the nearest city. At night I would sleep there on the benches, and during the day you could find me walking in the market area. I would find food in garbage cans, left by the venders in the market. Some of the venders who sold fruit would give me some of their extras, and I would store it up to last each day. Months had passed. I would go to the bus station bathroom and wash myself. I would have the same old clothes on even after washing. This made me very angry at anyone who had nice clothes. If I wasn't at the bus station, I would go to the train station. There were more people at the train station, and I could usually find better food to eat there.

At this time in my life I would spend much time in the stores looking at all the merchandise. I was dirty and was always asked to leave the stores. I remember I became a window shopper. I would tell myself, some day I would have those clothes to wear. I would pretend I was wearing those clothes as I walked back and forth in front of the stores. In my mind I was rich and dressed like a millionaire. I often saw myself reflected in the windows, and although I was dirty, I saw myself as a beauty princess.

I would sleep, in the train station much of the time. Each night after midnight, this man would be going home from work. Each night he would just look at me. Could it be he cared about me? One night he came in the train station and asked, "Where are you going?" I glanced up at the train schedule and chose the next destination on the schedule. I told him I was going to the town that was next on the train schedule. He then told me he was going to that same town, and then asked, "Why don't you get on the train if that's where you are going?" And, then he asked, "How do you get to the town if you never get on the train?" But I had no answer. Surely, he knew that I was lying, yet he pretended to believe me. The next day I went to a different place in the station to sleep so he wouldn't see me. I slept behind the train station from that day on, for he came to the station every night and I wanted to avoid his questions.

CHAPTER 3

THE RAPE

I was 14 years old, sleeping behind the train station in the alley, when I heard footsteps coming. I thought maybe somebody was just passing by, as often would happen. In a train station people are coming and going all the time. But this person came closer and closer to where I was. Surely they would not see me and just pass by, as had happened many times before when I slept at this train station. People often just pass by, never paying attention to a child sleeping in an alley. This night my life would change, for I was not that lucky. It was after midnight and the last train had long since gone. This stranger grabbed hold of me. I started screaming, hoping someone would hear me. He placed his hand over my mouth. I remember I was struggling. I could not breathe, I thought he was going to kill me.

He proceeded to rape me. I tried to scream, but nothing would come out of my mouth. I was in pain. I was terrified, as you can imagine. I was trying to figure out what in the world this man was doing to me. I knew nothing about sex. I was thinking the man was trying to kill me. For the first time in my life I had no control, and I could not run or hide. I was telling myself; *let me just die, please let me just die.* When he was finished, he just got up and walked away as if nothing happened. It seemed as if he took my life with him as he left, leaving me there to die.

At that moment I was completely surrounded with fear and emotion. I did not know what to do. I didn't know where to go, or if I should tell anyone. I didn't know what I would tell them, even if I was to tell. How would I explain what just happened? I did not think anyone would believe me if I told them anyway, because of all the rejection I had had in my life. I felt like I had tried to tell my mother and my daddy how I felt before, and they didn't care enough to believe me. Why would anybody else care or believe me? I did not know at this time what rape was. The fear of the moment and what just happened blocked my mind. I was thinking, why would anyone hurt a child who was sleeping in the street like this? I was only seeking a place to sleep. I was not expecting, wanting, or thinking somebody would attack me. This man took my peace and my feeling of safety as well as my sleep from me. Before this night I was not afraid to sleep. Now I was afraid to close my eyes for fear it would happen again. Would I ever feel safe again? Would I ever sleep again? There was so much fear and torment in my mind. I ventured into the train station, into the bathroom to try to wash myself. I tried to wash the blood from my body and the tears from my face. I felt disgusting. He left something inside of me and I could not wash it out. There are no words to describe the horrible feeling that I had; and I would have to live with these feelings as a little child, and possibly my whole life.

I kept asking myself; how could anyone want to hurt a little child. I had been in the streets the better part of my life. My life was not easy, but I had made it through rejection, loneliness, disappointments, beatings, hunger, and abandonment and survived it all. I thought about my daddy, if he had only been here, this would not have happened. At this time I began to develop a hatred for my father. I didn't want him in my life anymore. Somehow it had to be his fault, because he was not there. I also began hating my grandmother and blaming her. She had taken me to my mother's house from which **I had to run away**. Here I was minding my own business, not hurting anyone, and I was viciously attacked. This stranger scarred me for the rest of my life. He robbed me of the love I had for my father and my grandmother, the only two people that I had ever loved in my whole life. This stranger had stolen that from me.

I remembered the cow I had talked to and slept next to in the barn. I wished the cow was here to talk to. I thought she could take this pain from me. I felt as if the cow was the only one that could understand me. Each time I would talk to the cow and tell her how I felt, she would just stand there and listen, never running away, never abandoning me. That cow had become my safe object, and the barn my safe place. I was safe in the barn with the cow where I could tell my secrets. I was not there now. I was at the train station. I'm asked myself, where can I go? Can I ever trust anyone again? I believed everybody would hurt me.

The hatred for my father started growing day by day. As you can imagine, I even began to curse my father, and I began to curse the day that I was born. I kept asking myself over and over, why was I even born? What am I doing here? Where am I going to go? Who's going to take care of me now? Who would want me? Days passed. I started pretending that it never happened, and that I was not messed up. I thought if I just forgot about it and never talk about it, it would go away. But it did not go away. Every time somebody would come close to me, the fear would rise up in me again. Each day it was a little worse. No matter where I went, no matter what I did, I never felt safe. I was always on the lookout, trusting nobody. From this time forward, I would sleep inside the train station where the lights would be on, or I would sleep in the lady's bathroom where I thought I would have a little protection. I would usually make sure I had somewhere to run if I needed to escape, staying awake all night sometimes, and sleeping during the day when I could.

I developed a hatred for every man that I saw. Each time I passed the train station I started feeling like I was being smothered and I could not breathe. I guess you would call it panic attacks. Day after day I thought to myself that sooner or later this disgusting feeling must go away. If I could just get enough soap and water and a towel, maybe I could wash it off and I would feel better. I found out later in life, no matter how much you try, you cannot scrub the filth of this world off you. You can't just wash away what someone has done to you. I thought; I would be full of fear and dirty for the rest of my life. In actuality I was, until the day that I received Christ Jesus as my Savior.

I usually hid from everybody except to go to the bathroom and wash myself. I didn't know what to do. If I spent time inside the station late at night the man who talked with me earlier might see me, and might ask about me again. One night I was coming out of the bathroom and sure enough, the man that I had been avoiding at this train station every day, the one who was going home from work each night, saw me, and he questioned me about where I was going again. He told me that he had two sons, a wife, and a daughter-in-law at home. He informed me he had talked to his wife about me, saying in a very caring, calm voice, that he knew I was homeless. He asked me if I would like to come and live with his family for a while. I wanted to run, simply because he was a man and I was scared of what he might do. He saw my fear and had seen me crying in the past, and I didn't trust anyone. He told me he was concerned that I slept at the train station, and was fearful of what might happen to me as a young girl there. I remember I just stood there frozen, thinking he could have hurt me before if that was his intent.

I thought about going home to my mother's, but decided against that since I would just get another beating. I hated my mother and wanted her to die, so I certainly didn't want to be around her or think about her. I looked around and saw there were lots of people getting on the train, including women and children, so I assumed I would be safe and could get help from one of the other passengers if needed. Since I had recently been raped, and felt surrounded with fear, I said yes, because I knew I needed to get out of the train station. I needed to get to a place where I might feel different, especially after what I had been through. So, I went with him that night. We rode for about an hour and a half on the train. Upon arriving at his house, it was very late. His wife greeted him at the door, and there I stood with him. She was a very kind woman and she welcomed me with open arms as we entered their house. I remember that she first gave me some food to eat, and then said I could meet the family in the morning. The man and his wife showed me where to sleep, and they went off to bed. Upon awaking in the morning, I was offered some clean clothes, so I washed and cleaned myself up, and was then introduced to the entire family.

His daughter-in-law asked me my name. She kept looking at me and said that I looked familiar. I kept saying to her, "I don't know." We talked for quite a while, and we got on the subject of where I was from. When I told her I was from Veleki Popovc she seemed surprised, and kept asking me a lot of questions that made me very uncomfortable. She asked me my father's name, and then my mother's name. Upon learning who my parents were, she looked at me with a glare and astonishment. She declared, "Oh my God! You are related to me." I asked how, and she responded, "Your mother and my mother are sisters." "You look just like your mother," she said. She saw me at my mother's house, as I was caring for the sheep. She said her mother and my mother would argue about the way she kept me out of the house and how she treated me.

I could tell by her excitement, that she was much more comfortable with this information than I was. I had never met this side of my family, so I didn't know if she was telling me the truth or not. With all I just went through I did not trust anyone. I didn't even know why I had come to this home to start with! That man at the station was basically a stranger to me, except that I saw him each night as he boarded the train for his ride home. Here I was in their house, talking about a family that could care less if I existed. She then told me some things about my mother. I knew she would not know these things if she was not truly related. She told me I had a sister, and told me my sisters name, she even knew how my mom had abandoned me. She knew all about that.

She gave me enough information, to assure me that we really were related, to convince me she wasn't making it up. I stayed with them for the next couple of weeks, when they finally asked me what my plans for my life were. These people were the first adults that I had spoken the entire truth to. I told them about my fears and rejections. They asked me if I would like to get married. My response was, "Who would want to marry me?"

They then informed me that they had a neighbor who had just come home from the Army. His mother was invited over to the house and began a conversation with me. She seemed to like me. The next day she brought her son to introduce him to me. They asked me if I would like to marry him. I thought, why not! I was not thinking about what marriage was, instead I thought, at least I would have a home, a roof over my head, and I would have somebody taking care of me that had food to eat. We made an agreement, and I moved into his home and became his wife. No marriage. *But that's the way they do in Yugoslavia.* At this time I was only 14 going on 15; not knowing anything about marriage or life. All I knew was rejection and now somebody was finally willing to feed me, give me a bed to sleep in, and act like they cared for me. I had not the slightest idea what I was getting into. I was not thinking about the consequences of such a decision, after what I had been through. I certainly was not thinking that he would be lying in the same bed with me.

A few months later I discovered that I was pregnant. I also discovered that my husband was just like my father. Alcohol and gambling were the center of his world. He had no intention of having a family, but here I was pregnant, and he was left with no choice. I was living in his house with his parents, his grandparents, and his sister, and he was out all night gambling, drinking, and coming home whenever he felt like coming home. He was beginning to dislike me, and began treating me as if I did not exist. I assumed he treated me this way because I was pregnant, and he did not like the idea of fatherhood at all. His plan was to not have children, and he had no intention of being tied down with responsibility. He wanted to be able to play, doing whatever he wanted to do.

During the pregnancy he informed me that he only married me because his parents insisted he marry me. Here it was; all happening again. I could tell that the other people in the household loved me and were happy that I was going to be having their grandchild, and their great-grandchild, yet I was being rejected by my husband, simply because I'm pregnant.

The day came for the child to be born. My husband had just come home from a three or four day drunk. I told him that I was in pain and thought I was ready to have the child. His response was, "That's your problem." I went to the doctor by myself, which entailed another train ride back to where the man had originally found me. I entered the hospital by myself, and sent word back home to his relatives that I was in the hospital having the baby.

That night I had my first child, a beautiful girl! "Zaklina." The next day my husband's parents came. I asked about my husband. His mom responded that she had no idea where he was. I was in the hospital for an entire week and my husband never came to see me or the baby. His mother started looking for him because the hospital refused to release me until my husband had signed papers. Since I was under age he must sign that the baby was his child, since we were not legally married. He finally showed up, but he refused to accept the baby as his child. The baby was a girl and he only wanted a boy, if he had to have a child at all.

He did however take us home from the hospital. But as we went home he kept his distance, walking in front of us or behind us. He wanted it to appear as if he was not with us. He was ashamed of not having a son. He dropped me off at the house and then he left. Three days later his mother found him in a bar gambling. She had an axe in her hand and told him she would kill him, because he had a family and was not taking care of them.

He came home, but he didn't stay very long. He made it very clear he did not care whether the baby had diapers or food or any care, if it had to come from him. My cousin, who lived close by, came by often to see me. She spent much time questioning my welfare and how things were. She was concerned and went to visit my father, telling him that I had a baby and how things were going for me.

My father came to visit. He was angry to find out that I had tied up with a drunken gambler, just like him. It also angered him that my husband did not care about me or the baby. This surprised me, for my father didn't seem to care about me either. Maybe now he realized I was not a little girl any longer. He told me he had a better place for me. I have plans to send me to America. He said, I could have a better life there for me and my daughter. I refused saying, "No, I'm not leaving, I want to stay here." I looked into my father's face for the first time since that ride to mother's house seven years earlier. I hated everything about him. My whole life was his fault. I thought to myself, now you want to come into my life when I don't need you anymore. Where were you when I needed a father, safety, love, care? I was full of anger and hatred, and only wanted my daughter in my life. I didn't need anyone else. It's too late to pretend he cared.

My father left that day, so I felt as if I won that discussion. As far as I was concerned I would stay here. My father returned in two weeks. This time he brought my step-mother with him and they demanded that I come and live with them. Now they were insisting they wanted me, but they did not want my daughter. I was afraid that I would be just like my mother, abandoning my "Zaklina." I was afraid people would see me like they saw her, deserting my child. Most importantly I did not want to leave my baby. My father took me forcefully that day from the house, promising me that he would build a room on his house for me and the baby, and that later we would come and get the baby, as soon as the room was finished.

I cried and cried, but I went with my father. I didn't have any choice or any rights as a woman in my communistic country. I left my daughter behind with my husband's family. I believed my father would come back and get her in a few weeks, just like he had promised me.

It was later explained to me that my father had pre-arranged a marriage for me in America. My father said that if I would go to America, I would have a much better life. He also said he would take my daughter, and arrange the papers for her to come to America and join me. I was only 17, trying to believe my father although he had not been honest with me in the past. I didn't have any rights. I didn't have the freedom or ability to make my own decisions because of my age and because I was a girl. He had all the legal rights to do as he pleased with me, in Yugoslavia.

Arranged marriages are normal in Yugoslavia, so I had to obey my father even though inside I was dying. Just thinking about leaving my daughter made me sick. That was what my mother did to me. I convinced myself that someday I would be with her. I thought if only she could come to America to be with me, I would be able to provide for her and take care of her like my father was saying. While I was waiting for my papers for America, I was not eating, not sleeping, losing weight, and worried about my baby; missing her. My father and step-mother loaned me out to a neighbor to work on their farm. In exchange for my work they would receive flour, wheat, and corn. I worked from 5 AM to 9 PM each day, seven days a week. I did this for several months waiting for my papers to be done. Most of my days were spent crying for my daughter, how I missed her so much. The woman I worked for would ask why I cried and I would explain what my father had done and about my daughter. She tried to comfort me with words about how she had relatives in America, and how much better off I would be there.

It took a long time for my paperwork to be completed, but somehow he did manage to get me a passport. This is a whole story by itself, as I traveled to America with an invalid passport and lived in America 35 years. I only recently obtained a legal passport from my own country. Understand that you need a citizen number to obtain a passport, and because of my mother and father's rejection they never registered me as a child, so I was never given a citizen number to identify me.

CHAPTER 4

COMING TO AMERICA

My father and I went to the embassy in Yugoslavia to get my visa for the United States of America. I remember the day. We had an appointment at 10:30 in the morning, it seemed like everyone in front of us was coming out from their appointment rejected for travel to the USA. I was very happy watching as they were rejecting everybody's application. I thought *surely they will reject me also.* I could not tell my father how glad I was, as one by one they came out rejected. He was hard set on me going to America, and I didn't know why. I would find out later my father had given me to a much older man in marriage.

When my name was called I went in for the appointment by myself, while my father stayed in the waiting room. The ambassador sitting behind the desk looked at me and said, "Why is it that you want to go to America? And for how long are you expecting to be there?" My response was, "I do not want to go to America. My father is making me go. He has arranged for this man to marry me there, but please, don't tell him I told you that." He then asked, "Why is he sending you if you don't want to go?" I told him why my father was sending me to America. This ambassador sat there just staring at me. I was thinking, I am positive he will reject my application. He will reject me, I kept telling myself, and I was happy to know that he was going to reject me. I would not have to explain anything to my father, but I simply could stay in Yugoslavia. "Listen to me," he said, "I think it would be a wonderful idea for you to go to America." I replied, "Absolutely not, I have a daughter here, and I don't want to leave her." His response was," You can bring your daughter to America very easily." I replied, "No,

I want to stay here with my daughter!" The ambassador kept going through the passport and the pictures we provided, looking very intently and then looking back at me.

He then asked me to tell him more about myself, but he kept staring into my eyes. I remember he had deep, bright blue eyes, and he kept saying, "Tell me about you." I did. I told him about my mother rejecting me. I told him about my father's drinking and gambling problem and leaving me at home by myself as a child. I told him about my daughter and how I got pregnant after having been given to a man. He responded to me, "Girl, the best thing for you is to go to America: it will be much better for you there. I know, trust me, you will be able to make money there and bring your child later. You will get a green card in America," he said. Further he said, "A green card will make it legal for you to stay and work in America and if you should have any problems, I will give you a number that you can call in America. A friend of mine is living there and he will help you with anything that you need."

I kept saying no, I didn't want to go to America, I wanted to stay there. I remember he leaned across this desk, looked me right in my eyes staring at me, and said; "You are going to America. It will be good for you; you will see when you get there." I was afraid of my father and what might happen if he found out I rejected the visa, so I was left with no choice and accepted the visa. As I was leaving the room he looked at me and said, "I will see you soon." I thought this meant we would have a later appointment. I did not understand that this was all there was for me to be on my way to America.

My father was thrilled to find out that I had gotten my visa and was going to America like he planned. On our way home, he told me how he had already made plans and taken steps to fill out the papers for my daughter Zaklina to come to America shortly after me. With his assurances, I was very content to go. At least I might have a life in America and my daughter would be coming soon, I thought to myself. A week later I was put on an airplane and sent to America, to Fort Lauderdale, Florida.

I never met the husband that I would have in America until I came to America. I saw a picture of this man, but the picture I saw was obviously taken of him when he was twenty some years younger. He looked young in the picture, but when I got to America, I discovered my father has given me to an older man.

Upon arrival in America, I didn't know anyone. I didn't speak a word of English. I had no idea what to expect, or where I was going. All I knew was that for the first time in my life, I was on an airplane. I was flying for what seemed like forever, and it seemed like the plane would never get there. When I arrived I was to be given to somebody in marriage whom I did not know the first thing about. I hadn't the slightest clue how he would treat me; it seemed to be the only choice I had.

I was in the airport, looking down from the second floor into the waiting room for arriving passengers. There stood a man with plastic flowers in his hands, with an older couple. I recognized the older man and woman, because I saw them before I left Yugoslavia, when they came to sell their property there, while I was at daddy's house. I did not recognize the man with them. My first words were, "Oh my god, let it be anybody but that man holding those flowers."

They had a picture of me. I was wearing a sign on the front of my shirt that read, hello, my name is Radica, I do not speak English. They knew it was me so they came over to me. What a shock. The man with the plastic flowers was the man that my father had sold or traded me to! I was to be married to this man and he was much older than me. He was the ugliest man that I had ever seen; I muttered in disgust. I had no idea just how ugly this man truly was, especially on the inside.

When we arrived at his house, it was obvious they were a very rich family. I told them about my daughter, my Zaklina, and asked the man I was to marry when we will bring my daughter to America. His response was, "Oh yes, of course I talked to your father about that." But it was all a lie. No one had any intention of bringing my daughter to America. The only plan was to get me out of Yugoslavia and bring me to America. I don't know whether my father made money off this deal or what he was thinking, but here I was in America, going to marry a man I didn't know, did not speak any English, and I did not know how I would survive. I had no family here except this man's mother and father, and they all lived in the same house.

I arrived in America on a Wednesday. Immediately I was put to work on Thursday morning. I was taken to work with my mother-in-law. We were going to clean houses and she would take the money for all the work. After work we would go home and it was explained to me that I would be expected to be the slave around the house. When we got home my work would not be done. My job was to clean, mow the grass, and do whatever needed to be done to make their life comfortable. It was also my job to cook the food, do the laundry, clean the house, and wash the cars.

Whatever was needed to be done it was expected of me that is what I was to do, simply for the privilege of having this old man as my husband.

A week later we were legally married. To this day I don't know how they arranged this. I was underage and my father did not sign for my marriage. So here I was in America and married. They immediately applied for my papers to stay in America and applied for my green card, and whatever else was needed. The very next morning, the day after the wedding, my husband started verbally abusing me. It would not take a week to discover there was no love in this marriage. The house law was laid down. I was not allowed to speak or voice an answer or do anything without his explicit permission. I was told that disobeying him would have bad consequences. Do as you're told; that's it. This is your life, you're in America now, and you should be happy, just do what you're told, don't ask questions, just obey me." Shortly after the marriage I asked him again, "When are we going to get my daughter?" His response to me was, "What daughter?" I can say that the whole time we were together, days, weeks, months, I had no feelings for this man at all. Each day was just survival, existing; yet I did have food and a bed.

CHAPTER 5

GETTING OUT

It had been only about a month into our marriage and at this point in my life I had been rejected by both parents, raped, given to men twice, and nothing was any better here in America. I decided that the only way to end this hurt was to kill myself. I was working with my mother-in-law Monday through Friday. I was under supervision 24 hours a day, seven days a week. Here I was again feeling as if I had to escape from this family. It was no better than the one I left in Yugoslavia. Again I had no one to help me. I was in a strange country suffering the abuse again. In the house they would speak Romanian so that I would not know what they were saying. They would only talk to me when they wanted me to do something.

My escape was to go into the bathroom, turn on the shower and pretend like I was taking a bath. I would sit on the toilet and there I would just curl up in a fetal position and cry. I thought: I have no reason to live. I began to cry out, "Oh God, oh God, what am I doing here? How could this happen to me? How could I have gone from what I had put up with already to this?" At least when I was home in Yugoslavia I knew the language; I could communicate with people if I wanted. Here I was so far from home. They talk behind my back and I didn't even know what they were saying unless they needed some work done.

My cry was continual, "Oh God, Oh God." (Let me say at this point I still had no idea who God was, or if there was a God). In Yugoslavia, at that time we were a communist nation. The only thing we ever heard about God were curse words. Nobody ever told me about God. I would have to find out He was there through all the things I had experienced. I will share later a dream or vision, I'm not sure which, so I will call it a vision. In my vision God appeared to me and made known to me some things that even after He showed them to me, I did not understand for many, many years.

The abuse escalated from verbal and mental abuse into physical abuse. I can't tell you how much I just wanted to die and end it all. This thought kept coming into my head; if I would just kill myself at least then it would all be over, I would have nothing to worry about, and at least I would have peace. The thought came so strong and it would come so often, that I began to like the idea. I began to make plans, even choosing a time to kill myself.

Finally the opportunity came. One day I was given a list of chores that I was to accomplish the next day. The family would all be going away for the day and I would be home alone. This was my opportunity. I had a large list of things that had to be done. I was happy as I decided this was going to be the day that I would finally end it all. They would return to the home, find my dead body, and it would be over. They even commented that evening about my happiness while doing the chores. They said they did not understand my happiness with all those chores they gave me to accomplish; but I knew this was going to be the last day of my life. That night, just as all the other nights I would go to bed, if my husband so much as touched me my skin would crawl. I was being violated. There was no love, there was no compassion, and we had nothing but the sexual act. I was being forced against my will. That night I could not stand him to touch me any longer. I felt like every time he touched me I was being raped again. That night I thought, one more night. Tomorrow I will do it; I will kill myself and it will all be over. I guess that night was the happiest night since I had come to America, since the day I met him at the airport, possibly from the day I was born. Deep inside I knew that the next day would be my last day on earth, and I was looking forward to it.

I heard a voice inside my head saying, "Go ahead and kill yourself. Nobody loves you. Your mother did not love you, your father did not love you, your husband does not love you, nobody cares for you. Just kill yourself, get it over with, and you will be happy." I believed this lie, and so I made my plans to do it. What a weight was seemingly lifted from my entire being as I looked to the thought, tomorrow this will end. Since I had no knowledge about God, Heaven, or Hell, it seemed natural and easy to think and act this way. I wondered what would happen to my soul and to my body if I died. Fear set in my spirit as I thought about it. I thought by killing myself, it would hurt my father for sending me to America. I was convinced this was the only way to end my pain, and remove the filthiness I felt inside from the abuse. I would constantly hear my husband telling me if I was to disobey him, he would throw me out in the street, destroy my passport, and do horrible things to me. I thought there is no other way out for me.

Content with my plan and happy with my decision I kept replaying over and over this voice, just kill yourself, get it over with, and you will finally be happy, then I fell asleep...

CHAPTER 6

THE VISION

I was lying in the bed. I don't remember exactly how long it was before I fell asleep. Remember that I was planning to take my life, but here I was, my husband next to me, and he asleep. I had finally fallen asleep when all of a sudden I was awakened by a strange touch. It felt as if somebody was tapping me on the shoulder. I thought it was my husband, so I pretended to be sleeping and tried to ignore it. But someone kept tapping me. Each time they would tap me it was harder and harder. I could hear my husband; he had turned away from me and was snoring. I soon realized it wasn't him tapping me. I thought it might be his mother as she would often wake me quietly so I could go to work. I opened my eyes. A huge Angel was over me and I was speechless. He held his finger over his mouth, signifying for me to keep silent. He placed his hand under my arm, and immediately a second Angel lifted up my other side.

I looked down into the room as I was rising, carried by the two Angels. I saw myself and my husband and we were both still sleeping in the bed: yet I was being taken up through the roof. I was carried by the Angels, each one holding me underneath my arms, lifting me up with them as we were being raised out of the building. The two Angels began singing. I remember their song. It was Glory, Glory to God in Heaven, the Almighty. I looked down to see if anybody was looking up at me. The higher we rose the more I could see below me, first my bedroom, and then the whole house. Suddenly I saw the whole state of Florida below me, and finally I saw entire earth. I was very concerned that somebody might be looking up under my pajamas and looking at me. The Angels then took me to a

39

place that looked like a large waiting room, like you might encounter at a hospital. The angels set me down in the waiting room, in the front row. I was sitting next to an old Indian man. I looked around the room and it is filled with all races of people, blacks, whites, Indians, young, and old, it seemed as if the room was just filled with all kinds of people from all areas of the world; people I had never seen before.

There was a room off to the side. It appeared as if there was an officer of authority in there. Each time they would call a name, that person would get up and go into the little office. I could see they were standing in front of a desk where a book was lying open, and there was a scale of balances there. Each time a person's name was called, they were beckoned into this room, and just when they were about to enter an Angel would suddenly appear beside them as they walked inside. This Angel was holding another book in his hand. There seemed to be a man behind the desk, but I never could see his face because of the glorious glow that was so very great in that room.

I saw many people go into this room before my name was called, each with an Angel by their side. Some of them would come back with the Angels, but for many of them the Angel would return back to the room alone. I watched as the people who did not return, would just fall thru the floor as if a trap door was in that room. Then the Angel would close his book and return to the waiting room. Each time the Angel returned alone he had a very disappointed look on his face.

I looked into the room wondering what was happening in there. I saw a finger going across pages of a book as if specifically searching for names. Then my name was called. I stood, went into the room, and stood before the person behind the desk. He called me by my name. He said, "Radica! It is not your time yet." I took a glance into the book which he had before him. Sure enough, I could see my name there on that page. At that moment an Angel appeared next to me. He was standing by my side. He also had a book in his hand so I thought to myself, what is going on with these books? He said again to me, in a very calm, collective, but also very powerful voice, "It is not your time." It was obvious there was a lot of love in this voice. He said to me, "It is not your time yet. You are going to go back, but you do not need to ask me ever again, why did I bring you here?" I thought to myself, I never asked you why I was here. Why would you tell me that? The Angel then walked me to another place. In my vision, we were walking down a long road with a beautiful green pasture beside the road. Flowers and trees were blooming everywhere, and all of a sudden

I experienced this overwhelming peace. It was inside me, yet all around me; it was all encompassing.

The Angel disappeared, and I was standing there alone. I began walking and I asked myself; what this place was. It was so wonderful. This was a beautiful place, and I could live here forever, I thought. This was so peaceful. Oh, I thought; "I'm dead." This must be heaven. WOW, I thought; I don't have to kill myself. I'm already dead!

Far off in the distance; I could hear people singing hallelujah, and Glory, Glory to God! Always saying glory more than hallelujah. I headed toward that voice, for there was something about that singing, it was drawing me nearer. I had to know who was singing. I had to know who they were singing to. I had to know where this singing was coming from. I had never experienced such an exciting, thrilling, yet drawing to what was going on. I was being drawn like a magnet to this worship, to this praise. I had to find out who was doing the singing, and why?

I looked on my right. The trees and flowers, it was as if they were singing, praising, even bowing down to this worship that was going on in front of me. I thought to myself, that this was so powerful. The whole earth should be hearing this. I wondered why I was the only one hearing this. As they said hallelujah, it was like an earthquake was hitting the earth. Everything and everyone that heard the word hallelujah was shaking. My thoughts were WOW! I know I must be dead, this can't be real! I just wanted to stay there. This could make me happy. For the first time in my life, I felt a peace like I had never experienced before. I did not care about anything or anyone, I just wanted to have that peace, and I wanted to stay where those words were coming from. I could not wait to get to that place.

Suddenly, I found myself in a fetal position crying again, "Oh My God, Oh My God, I kept saying, "What am I doing here? What's going on?" I cried. The next thing I remember I was being taken in a chariot. I was in the back of the chariot in a fetal position on the floor crying, "God, why am I here?" The man who was driving the chariot, then said to me, "Did not God tell you not to ask him that?" I responded, "There was a man behind the desk that said that, the man with the big book, he said that, but not God!" (I didn't know there was a God at this time yet) He answered, "Don't ask God again what you are doing here. Don't ask ever again."

I said to this the young man driving the chariot, "Who are you to tell me what I'm supposed to ask?" I then tried to cover myself up, because I realized I was still in my pajamas. I glared right into his eyes and then

I noticed they were bright blue. I asked him, "Who are you?" He looked straight at my face and said, "They call me Michael." I excitedly responded, "Michael, the Arch Angel?" He just looked at me and did not answer me. I said, "I know you. My father worships you once a year. I've seen your picture on my father's wall, but you don't look like your picture." He did not answer me.

We soon arrived at a bridge. It was an old bridge that was obviously falling apart. There were many pieces missing from the bottom of the bridge making it impossible to cross. It would be like walking across a swinging bridge with most of the walkway missing. I could hardly see the other side, it seemed like it was a bridge spanning a large ocean. Michael said to me, "I will see you on the other side." I asked, "What other side? There is no way to get to the other side. Why can't you see there is no way to cross on this bridge? The bridge is very narrow and very long," I said. He answered, "I will see you on the other side". I was now left alone and fear started to fill me inside; no peace, just fear.

Suddenly, standing next to me was the same Angel that had the book in his hands earlier in the glorious, glowing room where I was taken. Opening the book, He said to me, "I will ask you some questions, and if you tell me the truth you will be able to cross, using this bridge. There will be a light that comes on, and you will be able to cross." I responded to the Angel, "I am not able to cross this bridge neither is anybody else. I'm scared, and I don't swim. I can see smoke rising out of whatever this bridge is crossing.

I said to him, "I am not crossing this bridge!" He ignored my resistance to cross over, He was carrying a black book that looked like a Bible. He was reading this Book and speaking to me at the same time. He then asked me a question and there appeared in front of me one step of this bridge. He said, "Stand on that step." Based on His questions, it seemed as if I was telling the Angel about the sins I had committed, then a light came upon me and warmth came over me, and the fear was gone. There was light now in front of me, and He just kept reading and asking questions. Each time He would ask the question, I would tell the truth, and another step would appear on this pathway. In the book He held he showed me that, the answers were already written as a record. I guess He was trying to tell me I had to tell the truth. It had already been written down. I was afraid not to answer the truth to His questions. Here we were. I was answering the questions and progressing farther and farther along on this rickety bridge.

I could not see any one, but I could tell that the water below, far below this rickety bridge, was very dirty and it was bubbling like a volcano. I looked down, (I don't know why I did this) but I could see that the volcano was bubbling with blood. It was bubbling and bouncing all over. The Angel kept reading out of the book and asking me questions as we went along. I just answered each question and with each truthful answer the light would come on and we would go a little further. There was an unusual peace, even though below me, was a terrifying painful site.

We arrived at the middle of the bridge. He then said to me, "Look down." I said, "No, I looked down earlier, and it's too scary. I do not want to see what is down there. I'm afraid to look down again.' As if giving me an order, "Look down." He said in a most forceful voice. I looked down afraid to disobey Him.

I realized that if I did not answer His questions and do as He said, as He quoted from the book that looked like a Bible that the bridge would end, and I would fall into this crevice beneath me. It was obvious to me, as I looked down, that this place below, must be some place with horrible pain and torment, such as I have not seen nor experienced.

Note: I have experienced a lot of pain in my life, and it was obvious to me that what was going on below me was worse than anything I had experienced. I know now that I was looking into hell. My vision of hell might not be like yours, but if you check it out with Scripture you will see that Jesus Christ, through his Angel, gave me this vision to change my life.

When I looked down into this pit, it was a lake that seemed to be so deep. It appeared to me that it was a mixture of both flaming fire, bubbling blood, and yet there seemed to be water surrounding the outside of the pit. It was filthy, disgusting water that was boiling from the heat of the pit. I could see that there were people there. They were chained, yet I could tell that they were getting beaten. I could tell that some of them were being stabbed. I was aware they were getting stabbed over and over. I could see the blood, springing up out of the pit, and it seemed that everybody was trying to get out of there. Some of them were getting up out of the bubbling and fire, and hands were reaching out and grabbing them, stabbing them, dragging them back down. The blood was spilling everywhere. The pit was boiling. It was constant fire. People were screaming and yelling, such horror, such pain, such terror unlike anything I had ever heard or felt.

"Look down," He said. I said, "No, I'm afraid. I don't want to be there." The Angel said, "Look down, and do not forget what you see." Three times

He told me, "Don't ever forget this!" I said, "How could I forget this. It is horrible." I didn't want to be there, and I started crying ferociously. I had never been so afraid in my life. I had had some hard times in my life, places where fear gripped me, even seemingly rendered me immovable, but never like this! I was aware that this was not just about me anymore, but this was about people, all races and kinds of people. People who needed to be, saved just like me, from the horrors that they seemed to be chained to.

I cannot put into words the torment I saw going on in that place. It was so clear, so vivid, and yet, so unbelievable. I was very much aware that I never wanted to go there. I never wanted to see this place again. And yet the Angel said, "You must look." It seemed as if all the people that were in that pit were looking up at us. I could see they were chained down and were being stabbed with primitive weapons of all types, over and over. Blood was going everywhere. There seemed to be some awful beast, hovering over the pit and beating them, holding them down each time they rose up to the top of the boil that they were in. The beast was also under them, pulling them back down. I could see that they were expecting us to do something for them. I heard them screaming, begging," Please stop this, get me out of here, and help me! Please help me get me out of here." they screamed. There was nothing I could do. The Angel repeated, "Do not forget this." I cried, "How can anyone forget this?"

He continued reading the book. The bridge was building itself again, and I was not too interested in the questions anymore. I just wanted to get to the other side, to be out of that place. Whatever was at the end of this bridge had to be better than where I was standing! We arrived on the other side, and I looked back again. The bridge looked badly broken and it appeared as it did before we started crossing, and yet I had made it over. It was as if we had not even crossed over. It was as ragged and impossible to go back. It was like we never crossed over. I thought. I can still see the steam and the blood rising up out of that pit. I looked around and the Angel has disappeared. Suddenly I was standing in a place even more beautiful than the place I saw on the other side of the bridge.

I was now even closer to the singing and worship than I was before I started crossing the bridge. I was in a place where everything around me was more alive than I had ever experienced. The grass was much greener, and it had a three-dimensional color. It was as if life had taken on a new meaning. Everything around me was bursting with new life, new color, and excitement. The thing that kept attracting me to this place was the worship I heard. I heard the song, Glory, Glory, Glory to God, God Almighty. While one section is singing, glory, glory another section is singing Hallelujah, Hallelujah to God Most High, it was blending together like an orchestra. I stopped, I listened, and I just knew it was not very far off. I was almost there. Who were these people singing? I had to find out! I began to run toward the voices of the singing.

I found myself being sucked into the ground into a very large hole. I grabbed for anything on the side, trying to get myself out of this hole as I fell deeper and deeper. The more I tried to get out, the deeper I went down. I quickly realized that if I kept sinking, I was going to find myself back in that pit that I had just come over. I was filled with fear. I was on my knees, remembering that horrible pit, and those people who were in it. I started praying, "Oh God, Oh God, get me out of here please!" Here I was, on my knees praying to God, any God there was. I just knew there had to be somebody to help me. I kept praying, "Please God, please God, help me. I don't want to go to that pit. Can't you see that I don't want to go there? Please, can you help me out of this hole? I will do anything you say, just help me out, God," I begged.

From out of nowhere, I heard a train coming. I thought to myself, there were no train tracks. We walked over a bridge. But what did I care, as long as *I* got help getting out of there. With this train it would be okay, I thought. The hole started getting deeper and deeper and I was being pulled down. I knew I was getting closer and closer to that pit. It was as if at any moment I would be right there in the pit I just crossed over. Then I remembered the train, but the strange thing about this train, was it was very big, and black, and it stopped right over the hole where I was sinking!

I heard the door open. Oh, I was so happy. I thought someone is going to help me. Suddenly there appeared, a little man and I do mean a very little, very ugly man. He was a very dark being. He spoke to me, but it seemed that as he spoke the words would come out of his mouth and fall to the ground making no sound. Because of this, his words could not reach to where I was, and I could not hear what he saying. I was asking myself, what was he saying? I called out to him," Help me, Help me, please! Get me out of here." Because I was pleading for him to help me, I could now hear his words. He responded, "I will, I can get you out of here." He said, "Don't you realize your dead?" "Yes," I said," but I still need help to get out of this hole. I don't want to go to that dark place. I don't want to go to that pit over there. Those people over there, are burning and in pain," I cried. "I don't want to go there. Help me out of here, please! I pleaded."

He said, "I will give you anything you desire and I will send you back and give you your life back." "Since you're dead," he said, "there is one condition. All you have to do is bow down to me, and I will give you anything you desire." Here I was on my knees in this hole, afraid to move, calling out to a "God," any "God"; a "God" I didn't even know, and this ugly little man appears. He told me he can help me if I would just bow to him. I don't know where these words came from, but I responded, "I will never bow to you! I will only bow to God, only God!" He laughed at me, saying, "Where is your God now that you're dead? How is he going to help you? Where was your God, when your mother left you? Where was your God when she abused you? Where was your God when you were waiting for your father, and he never showed up?" he questioned.

He then said, "There is no God. I am the only one that can help you," he said. "Think back on your life. He hesitated a moment and said, "You will surely see there is no God. Where was he?" again he questioned. It was as if every dirty thing in my life that had ever happened, was brought before my face as he said, "All you must do is bow to me, and I can make you free."

Something inside of me, I didn't even know what it was, (I know what it was now, but I did not know then) it was calling out from inside of me," Please God, Please God, please help me." I kept saying it over and over. That ugly little man kept saying; "There is no God. I told you, I'm the only one." I was trying my best to just ignore him, as I kept praying, crying out to God. The ugly man asked me, "Why are you calling on God? He is not here, there is no God, but I'm here to help you. All you have to do is bow to me, and I will help you out," he said. He then told me to stop praying, but I just kept praying anyway.

I don't know where the words came from. I certainly did not know them on my own. They were not my words, but I responded in defiance to this very little, very ugly man, "I will never bow to you, never. Only to God, and God only!" "Okay", he said. Then he reached into the train and pulled a smaller object of himself and set it down beside him. I don't know why, but I noticed it was on his right side. He said, "Okay, If you will not bow to me, maybe you will bow to my son. If you bow to my son, I will set you free." I hear him speaking, but I was trying to ignore him. I was still praying, hoping that God would show up and get me out of there. I said, "Get away from me, and take your son with you. I will never bow to you, the only person I will ever bow to, (I was pounding myself on the chest) the only person I will bow to is God's Son and Him only!"

Note: At this point in my life I had never heard that God had a son by the name of Jesus. I do not know where those words came from in my vision. I am only relating what actually happened and what was actually said.

When I declared that I would bow to God's Son and only God's Son, the very little, very ugly (devil) man, and his son, and their train disappeared. I was still on my knees asking God, "Who was that ugly person?" I continued praying to God, saying, "I will bow only to you." The hole started filling in by itself, and I realized that I was being lifted back up to the top of the hole where I started. I looked around and saw that I was standing at the top again. The hole I had just been in was no longer a hole; it was gone. I looked straight in front of me and there stood the Angel Michael.

Michael said to me, "You are going back." I reminded him, "That's what the man at the desk in the beginning, said". Michael then told me," It is not your time yet." I reminded him," That's what the man at the desk said, also." He said to me, "Don't ever ask God why you're here. You will find your purpose, why I brought you here, and what He has planned for you."

Then the Angel Michael said:

"I was sent to your home country to bring you to the United States, because: God has a plan and a purpose for your life. You are going to go back, and you are going to live to be 89. You don't even know this, but you are pregnant right now. You are going to have a son, and, his name will be Simon. Then he took his right hand as if swinging it out, and pointed in a specific direction saying, "this is his uniform." (I then saw a police uniform) "You will also have a daughter her name will be Savanah." He then swung his hand again. (This time I saw a nursing uniform). "Your husband will be very abusive. You will have a miscarriage and a stroke on the left side of your body. You are also going to have another daughter and her name will be Angela." Again swinging his hand, (I saw schoolchildren gathered around a teacher)." You will have a second stroke, again on your left side, and at this time even the doctors will tell you it is over for you. The doctors will say you will not walk or be able to speak, but you will survive it."

The Angel Michael continued:

"You will continue to suffer physical abuse from your husband, and you will get pregnant again. This Son, will be called Nathan. When He swung his arm this time, he specifically said, "This is your son," with a very strong power in his voice. I looked. I saw this skinny, tall young man, wearing what looked like a military uniform, blue in color. He was standing up holding a large book in his hand. There were thousands of people gathered around him, sitting in the grass, listening to him. He was pointing to the sky while reading from the book. Your son saved all these men. I asked, "In the Army?" It was as if my son was speaking to them from a black book, and the Angel said, "He saved their lives." (Wow, I remember thinking what a beautiful young man he is).

"Your husband will leave you with these children with nothing, but you will be happy that he is gone, because of the abuse. Don't worry. Remember the God that you were just praying to when you were in the hole. Remember the Son that you said you would only bow to. Do not forget that. When the time comes and you're in trouble, remember the God that you were praying to when you were in the hole. That same God, and his Son, will get you out of any trouble you get into. You must remember only to bow to him and him only. Do not be calling to me and do not pray to me. Pray only to God and God only; do not forget this, when trouble comes your way. The God that you said was in you, he will help you. Do not bow to me, do not worship me; but one day when you think you're in serious trouble, you call out to God, through his Son. You say to God, "I am in trouble, please send Michael; I need help." He then snapped his fingers, blew over me, and said, "I will be there, but you have to ask God for me. You cannot pray to me, you cannot call to me; you have to go through God. He is the one who brought you out of the hole. Do not forget this. He is the only one you should pray to, bow to, and the Son you said was in you, He is the only one."

You might think that after having this fantastic vision my life would have turned completely around. You might even think that I could avoid some of those things that I was shown, especially the beatings and abuse; but: No. To tell the truth, I told the vision to my mother-in- law, and she told the family. They thought I had lost my mind. I was made to see an Orthodox priest, who took me aside and asked me many questions. He asked me if I was trying to kill myself. I lied and told him I was fine, so he would not tell the family. He thought I had tried to commit suicide, but when I denied it, he then changed his opinion and decided God must have been telling me something. He also said God must have a plan for me.

I told him this was not some God, it was an Angel. Having heard this he assured the family that I was not going to kill myself, nor had I tried. He passed it off as a dream, telling them not to worry. However, privately he told me not to forget the vision. He was sure it was from God. He said, God was telling me something. I no longer had any desire to kill myself. I don't know what happened, but it no longer was in my mind. A few days passed and I totally forgot the vision as I had forgotten all my childhood dreams. It was gone and not to be remembered, as far as I was concerned.

CHAPTER 7

BACK TO MY LIFE

My life went on just as the vision showed me. I was indeed pregnant at the time of the vision. When it was time for the birth, sure enough, I had a boy. I named him Simon not because I remembered the vision, but because of his father's brother who had died. I named him after him. As far as I was concerned, that was why I named him Simon. Shortly thereafter my husband started abusing me physically again. He always had a jealous spirit and it would only increase. If I would talk to anybody, I would be in trouble. If, while driving in the car, God forbid we stopped at a red light and a man just happened to be in the car next to us, and if I should look in the direction of the other man, my husband would often beat me, accusing me of having an affair with that man. He thought I was having an affair, because, according to him, I would not be looking otherwise. He would often chase the car down, stop the car, and ask the man if he knew me. Regardless of how they answered him, he always thought they were lying and would take it out on me.

My Zaklina was about five years old. I had not seen her since being sent to the USA. I heard that my father had an accident, so I went home to Yugoslavia for a little visit; mostly to check on my daughter and see how she was doing. I found her to be very happy, satisfied, and joyful. She had just started the school year and it seemed she had everything she needed, except of course, her mommy. I asked her if she knew who I was, and she said, "Yes! You're my mommy. Grandma shows me pictures of you all the time."

It was common in the country of Yugoslavia that parents would often leave their children with the grandparents to raise them, as families there are usually very close. Two or three generations of families often live in the same house. Parents would often go to other countries for employment, leaving the grandparents to raise the children. It was not easy to find a good job in Yugoslavia, so parents would often go to France, Germany, Austria, Australia, or any country where work was available. They would seek employment and send money home, or come home occasionally, as money would make it possible. When parents moved out of the home, it was customary to leave the firstborn behind to be raised by the grandparents. They would also be the inheritor of the family wealth, usually house and land. It was also customary that the firstborn, whether male or female, would bring their partner for marriage back home to live in the house. In Yugoslavia, families would often build a new house for each generation. They would leave the new house with the property for the next generation. This still goes on today.

There are no nursing homes available in Yugoslavia. The firstborn is expected to take care of their relatives and the family house in order to gain the inheritance. While I was in Yugoslavia, I went to visit my grandmother with my little Zaklina. My grandmother was blind by now, but somehow she knew when I came into the room. She told me she could smell me and she could tell by the way I walked. She never forgot my steps. I never told my grandmother about the abuse in America. She asked about my life, and I said everything was great. I was ashamed, and in my country it is unacceptable to tell anything bad about your family. So, I pretended everything was good even though Grandma knew how I was raised. I wanted my grandmother to think that in America everything was going great, so she would not worry about me. During my two week stay, I looked for answers from my mother and father. My dad explained to me that he had tried to mend relationships with my mom after she left him. He said he had gone after her and she told him she had made a mistake to marry him. She told my dad she did not want to be poor all her life and that she wanted a better life than he could give her. My dad said she desired a better life than he was willing to provide. I had a great time with my father while I was there. During my stay my father did not drink. I don't know why he didn't drink, but I was glad he didn't. It made my visit joyful. My father and I rode around on his motorcycle and he took me to different restaurants where we would eat and talk. It was so exciting for me to spend this time with him.

I also had the privilege of taking my little Zaklina shopping. She spent these two weeks with me and we went to the store, and I bought her new clothes and new shoes. Not because she needed them, I just wanted to buy something for her. I remember her one request. She wanted a pair of leotards to match her new shoes. They had to be fancy, (you know how girls are). She wanted to look like people you see on TV. It was surprising to me, but my husband actually gave me money to buy gifts for the family in Yugoslavia. He also paid for my tickets. His brother had died earlier, in Yugoslavia, and he wanted me to visit his brother's grave, place some flowers on it, and clean it up. After two weeks, I came back home to the USA feeling my father loved me, but realizing that earlier in life the alcohol kept him from being able to show it. I was also at peace. Zaklina was well cared for.

I came back home to my husband. He was very controlling, even trying to control what I thought. I was never allowed to make a decision on my own or go anywhere by myself. I was told when to go to sleep, when to take a bath, how to do everything in my life. It was almost as if I was a little child being ordered around. Of course, after each of the beatings, he did what most abusers do, he would apologize, cry, and tell me how sorry he was, making promises to never do it again. Two or three days later it would start again, again he would apologize, and then threatened to send me back home, having me deported. He took my green card and all my legal papers and hid them from me. This was another way of controlling me. Without my legal papers, it would be impossible for me to leave or get any work.

It wasn't long before I was pregnant again. This time the abuse took place during the pregnancy. When the baby was born, she was a beautiful girl. I named her Savanah after my husband's mother. Again, I did not remember anything about the vision. It was simply naming the children after his family, as far I was concerned. This is important to me. Later on I will show you how God had his hand in my life, and I did not know God was controlling this. I did not know I was fulfilling the vision I had seen, yet this would be made clear to me many years later. As you can imagine, the abuse increased again. Each time it would progress a little worse, a little more severe, a little more often, as all abuse does.

I stayed with this man because of the children. Here I was in a strange country. I still can't speak English, and they speak the Romanian language in the house. I was trapped but at least I had a place to live. In my heart I believed all women suffer this same lifestyle. It certainly was the only life

I ever knew, so I thought I was living a normal life. I believed in my mind that this must be real life, this is how it was to be, and maybe my life was meant to be like this.

Savanah was just a few months old, when one day he was beating me and accusing me of cheating and having affairs, loving other men, even actors on TV if I watched any. I was trying to learn English by repeating what the TV actors would say. He would accuse me of having an affair with the TV people. He would abuse me and beat me up because of the TV. He would say if I wasn't having an affair, I would not be repeating what they said. I did not even know what I was saying, I was just repeating the words, trying to learn the language.

The stress was getting harder and harder on me. I was in the house, when I experienced a stroke coming on. There was tightness in my chest; I seemed not to be able to breathe. I was very dizzy and passed out on the floor. The next thing I remembered, I was in the hospital emergency room. My husband had called the ambulance. I was in the hospital, unable to speak, and I could not move my left side at all. I was semi- unconscious, yet I could hear them talking over me. I heard the doctor, say to my husband, "you had better prepare yourself; she probably is not going to come out of this." Because of the stroke, my mouth was pulled to the side, my left arm would not move, my left leg would not move, and I could not respond in any way. Inside I was talking to myself and I knew what was going on around me. I was trying to tell them, I'm going to be fine. I tried to say, I was going to get up, but nothing was coming out of my mouth.

They brought in a Chinese doctor who gave me a shot of some type. I was told later it was an experimental drug. Thank God it worked. First I regained use of my leg, then my arm. Soon I was able to speak, though not very clearly, but I was able to say words. Later I was discharged and went back home. My life seemed like a hell, I had a feeling that it would never end. Another year passed and I am pregnant again, for the third time. I thought, "Oh my, I can't even take care of the kids that I have now and I'm having another one."

I went to the hospital to deliver this child. What a surprise, another girl, just like the vision. I named this child, Angela after my husband's grandmother. Angela was three months old and again came the abuse. You might ask yourself, why would I put up with it? Try to understand, when you're a stranger in a strange land living with strange people that are not your own family, with no connection to your own family back home, you just put up with it thinking it is normal life and you have no choice. If you have never had a better life, you think everyone has it like this. Besides, where would I go? I had no money, no passport, and no job. I worked for his family for free. Where would I go? Soon we moved from Florida to New York. The move was under the pretense that he wanted to be near his other children. I found this out after we had been married for some time. His previous wife called about child support and he had to tell me. After we moved he had no contact with his children, nor did he support them. Life with him was just one lie after another.

The abuse was so obvious that one of the neighbors called the police. When they arrived the police told me I had to leave to stop his abuse. I told the officer I had no place to go. He said they would take me to a shelter where I would be safe. I agreed, so I and little Angela went to the shelter. Simon and Savanah were in Hollywood, Florida, visiting their Grandma and grandpa. They had been there for Christmas and this was in early January. I was in the shelter for three or four days and I realized I needed some money to pay for formula and baby things that were not provided by the shelter. I called home to see if I could get some money, his answer was, "If you tell anybody about the abuse, I will kill you." So, I denied the abuse.

I stayed in the shelter for a short period of time. I remember walking across the street to a coffee shop. There was a very tall man sitting there in the coffee shop. He asked me if I was okay, and if I was from the shelter. When I said yes, he just handed me some money. I used the money to buy a cup of coffee, some formula and some diapers for the baby, but they didn't last very long. A few days passed and I called home again. My husband asked me not to stay away. "Please come home," he said, "I'm sorry. I will never hit you again." Just more lies, but what was I to do. The people in the shelter told me to get my passport, and then they could help me find a job. When I asked him for my passport, he refused to give it to me. That was his way of controlling me.

I went back home soon after that. I just made peace with myself again that this was the way life would be. I would do what I could to protect my children, and I would just live there. I guess I should say just exist there; never knowing what would happen from day to day when he would return from work.

A few months passed and I discovered I was pregnant again. This time I lost the baby to a miscarriage. I was kind of glad that I was not having this baby, because he was abusive to the three children we already had. The children were not allowed to play when he was at home. They were not even allowed to be out of bed when he was home. By the time he came home, at six o'clock, they had to be washed and already in bed. He did not want to see them, and he definitely did not want to hear them. I would allow the children to play in their bedrooms, but I would always tell them they had to be very quiet, because their father would blow up if they made any noise; but they knew that already. My children had already witnessed the abuse. They would hear him yelling and screaming at me, and often they would cry, not understanding what was going on. I did not want another child to be in this environment. I did not know at the time how much my children actually witnessed or understood, but since becoming adults, I have seen the damage and the results of what they saw and understood as children. I thought it was hidden. I did my best to hide it so that they would not see it.

I would pretend he was a good husband in front of them. Later, they told me they would peek through the door and watch. My youngest daughter remembers seeing her father hold a knife to my throat, threatening me. I think to this day she still has issues with that. Sometimes they would call the police, or they would open the window and call to the neighbors to call the police. It was not a good scene at my house. My children told me later that they would gather in the room and pray for me. They would even ask God to save my life. I don't know where they learned to pray. I guess when you're in desperate need, even if you don't know God, you call out to him. And that's what they did.

My children would often ask me, "Mommy, why do we have to go to bed so early? It's still light outside; other kids are playing." I would just tell them, their father was coming home, and he was very tired. He's worked very hard and he had to get some rest. This was the everyday excuse. I think they knew I was not telling the truth. I would have my children run to their bedroom as soon as they heard daddy coming and pretend they were asleep, because he would often punish them if he found them not sleeping. It was very plain to me that he wanted no relationship with his children. Today my children know their father never wanted them and never wanted to be around them. I don't know why, but I always told my children you must respect your father. "He is your father no matter what he does," I told them.

I think back today, and it brings great hurt, to know that I allowed my children to suffer and go through all they went through. I did not know what I could do to protect them and myself. I did not know in America that there were laws against abuse. In my country of Yugoslavia, women had no rights at all at this time. Men could do with them as they desire; women were just a possession, servants to satisfy the men, property to be traded and sold. There was no such thing as rights or privileges for women. I'm happy to say today laws exist in Yugoslavia that allow women to have rights and protection. They're even taught how to defend themselves, both legally and physically.

I remember a particular trip to the store. It was a few days before Easter and I was looking for dresses for the girls. There happened to be a man in the store with his wife and his children. This man was looking at us smiling, and my husband got angry, jealous, and started accusing me of coming to the store to meet this man. He walked over to the man, yelling, "I know why you're here," the stranger responded, "Yes, I'm here with my wife, and were buying clothes for the kids." My husband proceeded to curse at him, saying, "No you're here to meet my wife. I saw the way you were smiling at her and looking at her." He responded with, "Sir, I don't even know your wife. I've never seen her before. I smile at everybody, but I was really smiling at your children. They are so cute".

My husband then dragged me and the kids out of the store. We never bought any dresses that year. In the car I started having a panic attack and I could not breathe. The closer we got to home, the worse it was getting. I asked my husband to stop at the drug store so I could get something for it. He stopped in front of a small drugstore, parking directly in front of the door. There were a few people in front of me in the line. He was watching every move I made from the car. There was a very tall man standing in front of me. He turned to me, knowing nothing about me, and said, "Don't worry, ma'am, everything's going to be okay." I thought this man said this because he had heard me breathing hard and it was obvious I was in pain. Upon saying this, the man stepped out of line, left his merchandise, and walking out of the store.

Another man came up behind me and made a comment to me about the line being so long and slow. I turned and said, "Oh! Yes." My husband was watching and thought I was flirting with the man. I could see him getting out of the car. He came in, and started a fight. In front of everybody, he said that I was pretending to have pain so that I could come here and meet this man.

The more he spoke the worse I felt. I passed out on the floor, and the man behind me called an ambulance. I heard the conversation; the pharmacist was trying to take care of me, along with somebody else in the store. I heard them call for a brownbag, I was hyper-ventilating; he said, Then placed the bag on my face and kept telling me to breathe. "Everything will be okay, he said. The ambulance is on its way."

The children were in the car outside, I heard a man's voice saying; "What happened here?" Everyone in the line is explaining to him what they saw. "This woman is an abused woman; I saw when her husband walked in the store." "Fear came all over her face, when he started accusing her of having an affair." "She had a panic attack and fell on the floor," one of the customers said.

Someone in the store, upon hearing this, attacked my husband and started beating on him. I heard people saying, "Stop; stop; you'll kill him." I found out later that this police officer was the first responder. He had lost his own daughter a few months earlier, after her boyfriend beat her to death. I guess he had a flashback at that moment, but there was no way he was going to let my husband do this again. I heard this officer say to my husband, "this is somebody's child, and you're trying to kill her!" I remember thinking, no, I'm nobody's child, who do I have? Nobody would even know or care if I died right there. They took me to the local hospital.

In the hospital, I heard my daughter screaming, "Mommy, mommy, please come back. Don't leave us here." Again I found myself in the same hospital where I was before, and in the same condition. So they called the doctor that took care of me the first time. I could hear everything going on around me. I was completely aware of where I was, and what was going on. I heard all the conversations. I heard the nurses ask my husband, "Are you abusing her?" Of course he denied this. One nurse told him she was well trained in recognizing abuse. The officer that had hit my husband in the store showed up at the hospital, to finish up his report. He informed my husband that the next time he laid his hands on me, he said, "I will be there and it will be the last time you do it. You will not breathe anymore." He added with an angry voice, "You will not be alive anymore the next time. I had a scumbag like you take the life of my daughter, and I know how to handle you."

I remember someone called the chaplain from the hospital to come into the room. I was unconscious, but I could hear him praying for me. I heard him ask if I had children, and when they replied, yes, he told them to bring them over to me. The nurse thought it would not be good, but the chaplain said it would okay. "Bring her children close by her," the chaplain told the nurse. The doctor agreed, as he was monitoring my heart to see whether I would respond to my children's voices. I guess they were checking to see if my brain was working. When the children were standing beside me, the nurse said, "Look, Radica, your children are here." My heart started beating very fast, the doctor said, "She knows they are here. She's responding, this is good" My right hand was tied to a board with IV's in my arm and I tried to move my arm to find my children, to touch them. I remember the nurse took my little "Angela" and laid her on my chest. She then untied my right hand, I guess to see what I would do.

I remember trying to reach my arm over Angela to hold her, but it would not move. The nurse reached down and put my arm over little Angela, and tears started coming out of my eyes, Savanah, was standing next to me crying. I moved my hand from Angela and touched Savanah and I could tell they were surprised. I thought; I might be touching my children for the last time. In my head I kept hearing the man that was standing before me in the drugstore. His voice was so loud in my head, it was as if he was standing next to me. "Don't worry ma'am everything's going to be okay," he said. His words, echoing in my head, gave me hope. I know now that this man was probably speaking for God, for truly, I was going to be okay.

I immediately started making plans to go home, but the words were not coming out of my mouth. After they put me in my own room I would lay in the hospital for several days. They continuously checked on me and gave me medication. I was going to get up, there was a great awareness in me, and I was going home to my babies. For three days, in my room I was mentally making plans for getting up and getting out of that place. I heard the doctor tell my husband, that I may never completely recover and that I may not be able to walk or talk. We have to wait and see. In my heart, I was saying, "I'm going to get out of this place." Three days after being in my own room, I was just lying there, when I felt this heat come over my body. I was excessively warm. I took my right hand, and tried to uncover myself. I thought this heat must be from the medicine they gave me. They had injected me with some medicine just shortly before this. I used my right hand, to remove the blankets, and I sat up on my own, no one was in the room with me. I could feel my body loosening up, and I had the feeling that I had to get up. I got up and I took one step. I remember walking toward the nursing station, and everybody was looking at me like I'm not supposed to be walking. I laughed, and they saw me. They came running with a wheelchair, and called the doctor.

I remember several doctors came over. What are you doing? They asked. How did you get here? I remember laughing and saying to them, I could not speak well, but I was mumbling, "I'm going home. I'm looking for the papers to sign myself out. I want to go home." That day I signed myself out of the hospital. The doctor told me he would not be responsible for what might happen, because they were not discharging me, I was discharging myself.

Before I left the hospital, the doctors took the time to explain to me my situation. According to them, it was stress that I was under, and the abuse from my husband. They instructed me that if this was to happen again, I would have a very large chance of not making it through another episode. They told me I had to do something about it. I couldn't go on like that. I said okay, and signed myself out.

Upon leaving the hospital and seeing my children again, I was almost immediately restored. I later got in touch with the doctors to thank them for what they had done. They explained to me how amazed they were at what happened. My doctor called it a miracle. I had no idea what a miracle was, all I knew was I was feeling good again and back at home, back to my babies. My speech came back, my pain left, and I was back to normal. Whatever normal was!

One year later, I was pregnant again. This time I had another son, and I named him Nathan, after his father. I thought with a son named after him he would surely change and be proud of a son to carry his name. I was wrong. I decided I would raise my kids on my own, and when they are older, and grown up I would move away from this man. But at that very moment, this was my life, right or wrong this was my life.

CHAPTER 8

ANOTHER VISIT HOME

A few years passed. My Grandma was sick, and this time I would take the three children with me, Simon was living with his grandparents, so only Savanah, Angela, and Nathan would go. I explained to my mother-in-law how I needed to go home to see my Grandma, hoping she would convince my husband to buy me another ticket and let me go. Well, he did, and my children and I were on our way. We arrived at my father's house about eleven in the morning. We were there at my father's house only a few minutes, when my father left the room and there was a knock at the door.

The police were looking for my father. When I told them I was his daughter, they informed me that Grandma was dying, and if my father was to see her, he had to hurry. I took little Savanah and Angela and dad. We got into the police car and they drove us to where Grandma lived, about a two hour drive. When we arrived at Grandma's house, my Aunt was coming out of Grandma's room. (*Grandma's room was not in the house but in a small one room tool shed.*) I could see the shocked look on her face as she saw me. She told me how Grandma was having a conversation with a man that was not actually there, telling him over and over, "I know Radica will come." They thought she was delusional. As I entered the room, Grandma was telling the invisible man, "Radica will come, you must wait." This was the first time Grandma did not recognize me. She was totally blind, but always knew when I was there.

I reached out my hand, gently rubbing her cheek, "Radica, I knew you would come." she said. Grandma then questioned me about those freckles.

I explained how I covered them up with makeup, and she reminded me how I always hated them. I crawled up in the bed, lying next to her. She told me there was a man in the room waiting to take her somewhere. I asked if it was daddy. She said, "No! I don't think he will come." Then my father walked into the room. He had been waiting at the door. "Surprise," I said, "daddy is here." I could see my father crying, and I can tell Grandma was happy that he had come.

Grandma was one hundred years old and yet she never forgot my freckles. My father stood there, as Grandma had another conversation with the invisible man. He seemed to be in the corner. The police brought in my two daughters. Grandma was touching them on their faces, saying she remembered when I was little like them. She told Savanah how she could not care for me when I was a young girl, and I could tell it hurt her to say this. Grandma started arguing with the invisible man again. This she would go on to do many times.

I had about forty minutes with my Grandma that day. It's amazing what one remembers. She wanted water. "I'm so thirsty," she would say. My aunt refused to give her water saying Grandma would just wet the bed. "I will clean her," I volunteered, and then I gave her some nice cool water, holding her head up just a little.

"Let's go outside and talk." my father said, but I would not leave my Grandma's side. When he said that, I asked my father to go get a priest. That was customary in our country. My grandmother grabbed hold of my hand and said; "I don't want a priest. I didn't steal anything, I didn't break up anybody's family, I didn't kill anybody, and I have been a peacemaker. I don't need any priest," she went on. "I fed the hungry, I have been basically good all my life, especially to other people." She then said to me, as if giving me instruction, "Radica, do not break up people's homes, do not stay mad at nighttime, make peace. If you have the ability, help people who are low to get back up. Do good things to those around you." These words would follow me throughout my life, haunting me.

I thanked my grandmother for the things that she had done for me as a child. She informed me that after dropping me off at my mother's house, she had come back several times to check on me. She said she did not let me see her, but had checked on me, and had talked to my mother each time she came. She said it was getting dark in the room. I thought, she is blind, how would she know? My grandmother then died in my arms. I asked my dad, "She's dead isn't she?" When he said "Yes"; I told Grandma how sorry I was for the anger I had towards her for the rape. I didn't want her to hear me, but I wanted to clear my heart of the anger.

My father and I buried my grandmother the next day, about one thirty in the afternoon. The graveyard was fairly new, so Grandma was one of few to be buried there next to grandpa and her son. It is customary in my country to have a dinner after a burial with the rest of the family, but my father did not want to stay. We both went back to dad's house to be alone.

I explained to my father that I wanted to take my children over to see my mother. The next day we caught a bus over to mother's house. My sister and her husband were there, but my mother was not home. They said she was over at the other house, so my sister's husband left and went to find her. My mother came to the house. I remember the first thing she said, "What did you bring me? How many suitcases do you have?" Another custom of my country is when visiting a home, you bring a present. My mother did not hug or kiss me or my children. She said, "Sorry, I'm dirty." My mother was not dirty, she just had no emotion to us being there, and it was as if she didn't care.

I told my mother I left my suitcases at my father's house. This was a big mistake. She immediately started in on me about my dad. She went on to tell me that I left my possessions at his house so I wouldn't have to give her anything. The truth is, I had brought my mother some presents, a new sweater, some other clothing and a scarf. I also brought some food items, which also is taken to people's houses in Yugoslavia when visiting. I explained that I just came to visit. I wanted to show her my children and let her know I was okay.

I was there with my mother less than one hour, and my mother threw us out. She took my gifts, and tossed them out with us. We walked to the nearest bus station, me, little Nathan, Savanah, and Angela. We were standing there at the bus station for quite a while, and it was getting dark. It was cold and we were not prepared to be cast out like this. We were hungry. Nathan is just a baby, and my children were looking at me as if to say what do we do now mommy? A car went by and then backed up. The driver told us there would be no bus until seven o'clock the next morning. He offered to take us to a motel, and we accepted his offer.

We stayed in a motel for three days. I did not want my father to know what my mother had done. After the three days we returned back to daddy's house. I told him we had a good time and the visit was okay, but little Angela gave away our secret. She explained to my father that there was a goldfish pond at the room where we stayed, and he knew that was not my mother's house. A few days later we returned to America. All things considered, it was a good visit with my dad, he got to meet three of my children, and we buried Grandma. I was glad to see her and hear her voice again. My Grandma truly loved me.

CHAPTER 9

RELIEF IS COMING

I remember when Savanah was five years old. One day my husband was actually stomping on me, and hitting me. Savanah came up behind him with a large frying pan, and then proceeded to bop him over the head, declaring, "That's it. No more hitting of my mama." She called the police on him. When the police came to the house, the second officer, to respond to the scene was the same officer that came several years earlier. He had warned my husband that he had better be careful. He was going to be watching. He grabbed my husband, and slammed him up against the wall. He took his police club and beat the daylights out of him, and then took him away.

Of course my husband came back in a few days, and he was very quiet for the next few days. We soon moved to a new apartment, but he did not move his clothes into our new apartment. I knew something was going on when he refused to move his clothes into our apartment. He was taking a bath at the old apartment, when I went through his wallet. I stole five dollars from my husband, because at that time I had no money. I was terrified to take any more than that, and if he had caught me I would have suffered another beating. I had no idea that this would be the last time I saw him. He came out of the shower, got dressed, and left me a note saying he was leaving me. I was afraid, I had five dollars to my name, three children living with me and Simon living with his Grandparents; yet at the same time, I was also happy. I thought it would be better living single with my children on our own.

My husband had met someone else and was seeing her behind my back. I was unaware of the affair, but I soon found out. When I found out all I could feel was relief. Finally I knew why he did not move with us. Our arranged marriage came to an end, and I was happy about it. Shortly thereafter, I lost the apartment, for I could not afford the rent. I had no one to take care of the children. They were small, so I could not get a job. One day I was walking the streets with my children looking for a place to live. An elderly woman was sitting on the steps in front of where I believe she lived. As I passed by I simply said, "Hello." She started talking to my children. I found out this lady was from my very own country. She invited us in and this reminded me of the traditions in our home country. Others would always invite people into their homes and offer them something to eat and drink; not my family of course, but other families in our country. She made some food, which made me very happy. I told her about my husband, and how I had lost my apartment. She said, "This is convenient; there is an apartment right next to mine. It has just become available for rent." That night at five o'clock the landlady was coming to collect the rent. "Why don't you stick around and talk to her," she suggested.

I hung around the rest of the day until she came. I told her my situation, and she showed me the apartment. I asked the landlady, "Could you give me the apartment to live in for a few months without any money?" I added, "I will pay you later when I get a job." She looked at me as if I was nuts; no response, just looked. I could see that she was shocked that I would even ask such a thing. She then said, "Let me go outside and call my mother; she owns half of this building." I found out later that she did not actually call her mother. She just wanted to go outside. She came back, looked at me, and said, "Okay, this is the deal I will make. I will give you the apartment for a few months to help you, and you go find a job. There's no refrigerator there, but I will see if I can get you one." I would have been very happy to stay there without a refrigerator. I knew I could depend on the lady next door for some help because she was from my country, and in my country that's what decent people do, help those in need. Even though, I had not experienced this generosity in my childhood or at any point in my life, I remembered that this is the way people in my country treated others.

I moved into this apartment, we had no beds, just a few blankets and pillows, so we slept on blankets on the floor. I remember Savanah, asking, "Mommy, are we going to live like this all the time?" I looked at her, and said; "As long as you have a mommy things are going to get better. Don't worry mommy will get a job and it will get better," I assured her. The elderly lady next door offered to watch my children so I could start looking for a job. She even referred me to a place where she was sure I could get a job, it was in a restaurant. When I applied, the owner just looked at me. I looked around and all the waitresses looked so pretty with their cute uniforms, I looked like I was a homeless person, but I was looking for work.

I told the owner, I would be willing to do any job, even clean the toilets. I needed to feed my children. I told him my story, how I got the apartment and now I had to find a job so I could pay my rent. I explained to him that I had no food for my children. He agreed to give me a job cleaning the restaurant, and told me to come back the next day. He said I was to start at six in the evening, but I was there at four. I was an expert at cleaning, I had done this with my mother-in-law, without pay, for many years and I knew how to clean. As I was cleaning, I would watch the waitresses. I was going to come up with a way to get their job. I saw customers leaving large tips and I knew it was more than I was making, I was determined that I was going to be like them.

I was on the job only a week when I came to work early one day as I always did, and I asked the boss if I could seek a favor. I explained how I needed a little bit of money so I could buy beds for my children. I knew this was a big thing to ask, having only worked there one week. I also said I needed clothes, hinting so I can look good when I came to work. He asked me what I had in the apartment. I told him exactly what was there. I was embarrassed, but I had to tell the truth for my children's sake.

He looked at me kind of shocked, but he did not answer me. He just went down to the basement, where he had a room made ready to sleep if he so desired. I had assumed the answer was no since he did not respond. About half an hour later he came up from the basement, called me to the table, and had set me down. He handed me an envelope, saying, "Here's $5,000, and in exchange you must agree to work with me for one year. Do not even think about paying me this money back until the end of the year. At the end of the year I want you to pay me $100 a week until it's paid back." He then gave me a list of people that he knew that owned businesses. He said to tell each of them I worked for him, and tell them what I need and they would give it to me cheaper, he said. He then gave me three days off to take care of my business. He told me about somebody who had a car for sale, adding that I should buy it to take my children to school. I was so surprised and happy. I accomplished all this in one day, and went back to work the following day. He was shocked that I was there and didn't take the three days off.

For the first time in a long time my refrigerator was full. My children had plenty of food, a living room set, a bedroom set, TV, and a few games to play. We went from desperate poverty to having everything we ever wanted, all in one day, it seemed. I called my landlady to come and pick up the rent. She responded, "Already?" When she came to collect the other people's rent in the building, I offered her my rent. She would not take it. She said, "No I told you could have a few months free!"

I found out, that my landlady had compassion on me because she had gone through the same situation, with two children, earlier in her life. As I shared my story on the first day I met her, she was having a flashback of her own life. That was why she had to go outside. She said she had nobody to help her, but now she was able to help me. Thank God she helped me. I lived in this apartment for about four years, and always paid my rent on time. We had a very good relationship. I shall never forget how this woman helped me, reached out to my needs, and helped in a most difficult time of my life.

It didn't take long for me to become a waitress in this restaurant. I was very friendly with the people and I worked hard, made good tips, came to work early, and would stay late if needed. I can say that I never complained about my job. I was just thrilled that I had one, and it was a good job. Seven months after I started this job, I began to pay my boss back the money he had loaned me. I stayed with this business for many years, even after the business started to go downhill. He was forced to reduce our pay explaining there was not enough business to keep all of us working, but I stayed to help him just for the tips. I remembered how he helped me, and I wanted to return the favor.

My income was very low at this time. One day he asked me to drive him to a coffee shop. A conversation began with the man who owned the shop, his friend. He asked him to hire me. His friend agreed to hire me, so he turned to me and said, "You no longer work for me." He closed the business just a few days later, and I started working for his friend from that day forward.

One night while sitting at home alone with the children, there was a knock on the door. When I opened the door there was a police officer standing there. After he looked into my apartment and saw my children playing on the floor, he asked, "Are you Radica Milanovic?" I responded, "Yes, I am." He then said, "I am so sorry," he repeated, "I'm so sorry, I have to do this. These are your divorce papers." I must have scared him half to death. I jumped up and down, hugged him, and even kissed him on the cheek. I think I was kind of dancing, I was so happy. To me, this was great news. I hadn't seen my husband in quite some time. He already was living with the other woman, and this meant he was leaving me alone, I hadn't had a beating in quite a while; I was feeling pretty good. This chapter of my life was coming to an end, and I didn't have to do it; he ended it for me.

"Thank you," I said to the officer, "you have made my day." The kids were asking me why I was so happy, so I explained it all to them. They joined in the celebration as we danced around the room. I don't know if they really understood it, but Angela looked at me and said, "Mommy, you're not going to cry because of daddy any more, nobody's beating on you anymore, and we can stay up late at night, if we want to." I responded simply, "Yes honey, yes we can. We are now free," I said. "We don't have to worry any more".

Over the next few years, my son, Nathan, would ask me many times where his father was. "I want my father," Nathan would say. This brought back many memories of the times that I would cry for my own father. I knew how my son must have been feeling since I had been in those shoes myself. My son was having sessions of depression, he was acting up in school, skipping school, and it was obvious he was having a very difficult time dealing with how he missed his father.

I would talk to him many times, trying to explain things to him. How does one explain these things to a child? He soon became a teenager. As a teen my son started cutting himself and became suicidal. He would say things during these times that let me know he was doing it because of his father, the anger and the emptiness he felt because of the absence of his father. All through their childhood, from the day those divorce papers were delivered and even before, the children never received a birthday card, Christmas card, nothing from their father or even their grandparents for that matter.

Through the years, I would do everything I could to try to help my son to understand his value. I even had to put him into a hospital, because he was cutting himself and trying to kill himself. I think the spirits must be transferred, from one generation to the next. Here I was looking at my son, and he was facing some of the same issues I faced at his age. I was determined that I was going to protect him if I could. I explained to him that I would be his father and his mother, but somehow he still needed a father. I could see he had such a strong desire to be able to do things with a father, like the other children he knew. I could see him acting out his anger, beating up other children, causing problems, just to get attention; because he wasn't getting what he needed. I was being destroyed myself, just watching my son reacting to situations just like I had done at his age.

I had to make a change. I had to do what I could. I loved my son but, to tell the truth, I did not know what to do or how to do it. At one point I tried tough love. I put him out of the house I could not control what was going on, but that did not work either. After just a short time of staying with his friends, and sometimes sleeping on the street. I had to let him move back home. I could see the suffering, and I could see that we were suffering together trying to meet his needs. I had no clue what I was doing, or what I would do next. We tried counseling, but it did not work. We tried medication, but it did not work. I was hopelessly unaware of what I should do next. I had had enough of having enough. Once again problems overwhelmed me. I didn't know where to turn.

I found myself working all I could, but still not having enough money to pay my bills. I questioned myself; what was I to do? How was this all going to work out? At this point, I was doing all that I can. I'm even on welfare again, just trying to survive. I was working as a waitress for about a year, when I was introduced to the son of my employer. We began dating and it wasn't long before he told me he wanted to marry me. My fleshly heart was telling me this was the man for me, but oh, how wrong my flesh was! **Jeremiah 17:9 The heart is deceitful above all things, and desperately wicked: who can know it? (KJV)**

We were not yet married, and I was pregnant. He suggested an abortion declaring he did not want a child, so I decided I would have an abortion. I was looking for the easy way out of my situation. I felt guilt and shame as I was going to the clinic for the abortion. Upon arrival at the clinic, the street was crowded with protesters waiving signs and shouting loudly. I asked my boyfriend who those people were and he said, "They are just crazy people. Don't pay them any attention and don't look their direction." I was confused, yet inside I knew this was not right. I felt as if I had to abort this child. Inside the clinic, I was sitting next to a young girl, so I asked her what I was to expect and if it was her first time. She said, "Oh no, I've had many. It's fast and simple." After hearing this I felt less guilt. I asked who the people were outside and if they were always there, or did I just pick a bad day? She said, "No, they are always there. They are some sort or religious group. Just ignore them." Right then I didn't know whether to run or stay. Then she said, "Just get it over with, so you won't have to face them again." The truth was I just made a selfish and bad choice that day.

The abortion only took a few minutes and it was over. Or was it? Coming out of the clinic I remember seeing one sign that stuck in my mind. It read, **Jesus forgives all our sin**. After having the abortion, I would regret my decision, but it was too late. That few minute's procedure would stay with me for a lifetime. I would suffer guilt and shame greater than what I had before the abortion. Until after the abortion I did not consider "it" a human life. I believed the lie of the world. "It" was just a fetus, but now I was well aware I had taken a life, a child, my child. I could not forgive myself for having done this.

I went to work and for many days I would have flashbacks of the people standing outside the clinic. I would see their signs in my mind, and I could hear them yelling and crying, "Please don't." I thought I would never be like those people, interfering in others lives, out in the public. Several months passed. My boyfriend was living at his home and me at mine, and I found I was pregnant again. This time I made up my mind, I would not give up this child! I had suffered enough from that first abortion, and I would never do that again.

One day after my birthday, on October 4, 1995, my son was born. I will call him "Jason" to protect his identity and the identity of his father. Before Jason was born, I found out that his father was already married and his wife was also having a child. While working alone one day I had to answer the phone, and I was told that his wife was in the hospital having their baby. They were trying to reach him. I thought they must have the wrong number. I asked who they were talking about. When they called him by his last name it was obvious they were talking about my boyfriend!

When he came to the store, and I gave him the message, his secret was out. His face saddened. He was shocked that his double life was exposed. He left to be with his wife. My fleshly heart had deceived me again. I decided that I could not trust my heart any longer. When my son was born I took him home. Jason lived with me for five years, and his father would visit him from time to time. He also supported him. He made sure he had everything he needed. He kept trying to continue a relationship with me, but that was over.

We soon opened a restaurant and bar together, with the idea it would provide for our son. I was to be the sole manager, and he would come from time to time to visit. Money was no issue as we had plenty. I could have anything I wanted. Eventually I told him it must come to an end. I explained to him that I would allow him to be a father to our son, but he would be nothing in my life. It was over. I was moving on with my life. He gave me a sad story about how he was leaving his wife and wanted to marry me, but I remembered my grandmother's words on her dying bed. She said, "Do not break up anybody's home." If I had known that he was married our relationship would never have started. I now knew the truth. He was married, it was over, but he wanted to keep the relationship going. He would buy anything I wanted, trying to buy my love, but I was through with him. He had deceived me, and I would not trust him again.

It was not to long before he started threatening me with the child. He said he would take the child from me. I thought he was just bluffing. I discovered that he had three children with his wife, plus my son. I took Jason and moved to Michigan, leaving the business and everything behind. Several months passed, and I came back to New York to pick up my belongings from my house. That day he took our son and left. I thought he was going to get a burger for dinner, as he often had done. I thought he would come back shortly. He called later that day to tell me I would never see Jason again. He then took me to court and received full custody of Jason. His wealth would prove to be a wall of defense against me. He would send my court papers to a wrong address, and by the time I found out, the judge had already granted him full custody. For about four years I could only call and talk to Jason.

At some point his wife legally adopted my son Jason. I was told to not call their home anymore and when he is of age, he could find me if he wanted to. I know that day will come when I will have to explain all this to my son. I will have to explain how sorry I am, how much I have missed him. How much I wished to be next to him. I will tell him how much I love him. I can't wait to share with him the five years we spent together, and show him the videos of his first birthday, first steps, first dog, first Christmas, first Thanksgiving, and first Easter.

I provided all the things I never had as a child during those five years. When the day arrives that I meet him again, I will not be as my mother was. I will welcome him into my house and try to make up for all the years, as best I can. I can only hope and pray that somehow he knows how much I love him, and how much I miss him. Until then, I will watch him on his internet postings. He is becoming a fine young man. I saw his graduation and other posts of the family. The internet is my way of connecting with him. I know this way, I can respect his adoptive mother and avoid causing her any more pain. I thank God for her and the way she accepted my son as her own. I pray God's blessing and long life upon her for the love she gives to Jason.

Up to this point I had repeated many of the same lifestyle decisions as my parents. How scary it is to look back over my life and see the same patterns of life. I was repeating them over and over. I was fearful and confused, but there had to be a way to stop this cycle, but how? Where could I find help? How could I break this lifestyle? It was destroying me and I seemed to be unable to stop it.

In 2000, my son Nathan turned Gothic, deciding the only thing to wear was black. He wore chains, and you know the look of Goth. I knew I needed to find help for myself, because at this point, I thought I might hurt my own son. I would talk to him, but it didn't seem to change anything. I got to a point where I stayed home three days in a row, suffering from depression. I would close all the windows to make my bedroom as dark as I could. The last thing I wanted to see was any light. I was quickly falling into the trap of depression just like my son.

CHAPTER 10

MY CONVERSION

I had spent three days in depression, crying my eyes out while I looked back over my life. I kept asking the same question over and over again, "Why me?" How would I get out of this? Where would I go? How would I pay my bills? Three days of crying day and night, night and day, maybe I was feeling sorry for myself. No, I'm sure I was feeling sorry for myself. Life sucks, I thought. I was at the end of my rope, and there was no knot to tie. I didn't know where to turn. I was afraid what I might do, and that I might even hurt my own son. My son spent the same three days in his room, with his door locked. I was probably good that he did. When you're depressed, you might do something stupid, and later regret doing it.

I was feeling sorry for me, about my life, when suddenly I had this feeling inside of me. I didn't know what it is but it was a gentle voice saying, "There's a better way for you. There's a better life. You don't have to live like this." For the first time in my life, I was seeing myself. My life had been disgusting. I was actually feeling guilty about some things in my life. I felt dirty and unclean about the choices I had made in my life instead of blaming others for what they had done to me. I think this might have been the first time I feel as if I had done something wrong with my life.

I heard this voice saying, "There's something better for you." I saw my past, sinful things, the things I had done in my life, and I heard this voice saying, "This is not right. You cannot live like this." I realize now this was conviction over the things I had done, but at that time I did not know what it was. I was fighting it, trying to hold on to myself, trying to retain my sanity. I had to save myself, I thought.

After that the third day, I found myself lying on the floor with my face flat on the floor. I was crying uncontrollably as my past and all my sinful ways kept flashing thru my mind. It had been three days like this. All those bad things that I had done repeating, even haunting me, over and over. So on the third day, each time one of those thoughts was brought to mind, I started saying, "Oh God, I am so sorry." I would cry out to God with each memory, saying, "Oh God, I am sorry." I started to feel as if I was having a little release with each outburst. It was as if I was being forgiven, being set free from my past; but I did not know how or why.

Finally, I cried out, "God! If you can hear me, if you are real, would you please show yourself to me? I promise you," I said, "I will change, if you just show yourself real." I thought I would change myself, if I found out there was a God. I would have to. I don't remember how long I cried, but I remember I asked Him to forgive me for all those things that were brought to my mind. "Just show yourself to me," I said, totally unaware that He was doing just that; showing Himself to me, reminding me of the things I had done, so that I could confess them. The longer I lay there confessing, the better I felt. There was a peace that was taking over my life.

I heard another voice inside mocking me saying, "You're only feeling this because you've been crying for three days." I responded, "No, No, I definitely feel better." I got up off the floor, for the first time, I had to open the windows and blinds. I needed to let in the light to force out the darkness of the room. I remember the happiness I felt when I looked outside, and saw the light; the feelings that entered into me at that moment I shall never be able to describe.

I went upstairs to my son's room. I gently called him, "Honey, come down. Mommy's making dinner." He came down, as I was cooking we had a good conversation. He asked me several times, "What has happened to you?" He knew that I had been going through depression, for those three days. It was no new thing to him, for he also suffered depression, and he knew what it was like. He kept looking at me as we talked. I was so very happy. My son just kept starring at me. He said, "Mommy, you look different." I heard that other mocking voice saying, "Yes, because you've been crying like a crazy woman for three days." I just ignored it and I put on some soft music. My son and I talked all that evening. As we watched a movie together, it was obvious that a totally different spirit was in the house. My son and I were able to talk and seemed to understand each other; we could feel each other's compassion and pain. We were able to talk. It seemed that there were no barriers left.

It seemed as if the night went on and on and on, as we shared things that we had never shared before. I remembered my son looking at me the whole evening. He had this shocked look on his face. It was like he was looking through me. He was looking at me in a totally different way. We spent the next day together, and he kept asking me throughout the day, "Mom, are you okay?" Over and over, he would ask this question, so many times that day. I responded, "Of course I am OK. Why do you keep asking?" "Mom, are you sure you're okay," he just kept on and on.

Three days after this experience, he asked me again, "Mom, are you sure you're okay?" I looked at him and said, "Stop asking me. That's enough, what are you talking about?" My son then said to me, laughing, "Look at you, mom. You haven't cursed at me in three days, and something's changed." Prior to this day, I cursed, it seems, like every other word. Now for three days, though I was not even aware of it, I had not cursed. When my son said this to me, something inside felt like, WOW! But wait a minute, I thought, how could I have changed my language like that? It was like the words just disappeared out of my vocabulary. I could not understand this. When my son said this to me, I felt another wave of peace. I never experienced this kind of peace in my life before. I started laughing, and I was hugging my son, and saying, "I don't know; I don't know what happened, but I sure am happy."

My son left, to go off with some of his friends. He was also happy. It seemed as if he had a new mother. When he left I was there alone in the house. I thought to myself, I asked God to show me if He was real, I didn't ask him to change my language. I just asked him to show me if He was real. It suddenly dawned on me; God had shown me He is real by changing my language. He had cleaned up my mouth, by giving me a new love.

That night I was home alone and I suddenly realized that I had hope (which I'd never had before). I realized I had a life worth living. I was joyful and I began to flip through the TV channels. I remember finding a channel where there was a preacher. I remember his name still to this day. Dr. Charles Stanley from, In touch Ministries. He was telling people how much God loves them, and how God is so real, and that He will show up and make your life real if you just ask Him. He said that He will never push Himself on you, but He will show up if you repent of your sins and ask Him to show up. He talked that night about forgiveness. I could not understand, I didn't really want to understand. I was a baby Christian, just born again, and I did not want to understand forgiveness yet! At the end of the program, he said a prayer, and I remember repeating the prayer with him.

For the first time, from deep inside of myself, I was praying this prayer with this preacher on TV. "I repent of my sin, I ask you Jesus to come into my life, change me" he said, so I repeated it. "Change me Jesus and give me a new life," he said. I had no idea that from that moment on I truly would have new life. I thought those were just words that people said, but that night my whole life changed. I knew that God had forgiven me. I knew that I was saved. I didn't know how God did it, but I knew it happened. I've now been saved for 10 years. I still don't know how it happened, Oh, but I thank God that it did.

After this preacher was finished, I flipped to another channel. Another preacher was speaking about this forgiveness stuff. As he was speaking about forgiveness, it was really bothering me. I could not understand why I would have to forgive people who had done horrible things to me! Even though I had just experienced forgiveness from God for my sins, forgiving other people was what this preacher was talking about. I had to forgive other people for hurting me! Understand, I didn't know anything about God. I was a baby Christian.

I heard a small, calm voice inside me saying, "Radica, you have to forgive your mother. You have to forgive your father. You have to forgive your ex-husband, and you have to forgive your in-laws and everybody else that has hurt you." I said to myself, "Oh, no. I will never do that; I will never do that, not if I had 1 million years. I will not forgive my mother for not loving me or caring for me. I cannot forgive my father; he turned his back on me. I will not forgive my husband for what he did. I cannot forgive my in-laws." I had this conversation going on inside me, and again that still small voice said, "Radica, you have to forgive." This went on for some time, when I heard the voice say, "If you do not forgive them, I cannot forgive you."

My first thought was, what? I had just heard that preacher on TV say I'm forgiven. "I'm forgiven." I said, "The preacher said so." But that small, kind voice responded, "No you must forgive them." There was a battle going on inside me that I did not understand.

CHAPTER 11

FORGIVING OTHERS

My process of forgiving my mother and father was long, drawn out, and emotional. I had a lengthy argument or discussion with God. I was mad at Him for even suggesting I had to forgive them. Yet, He kept telling me, by that voice inside, that I had to forgive them in order to be forgiven myself. I remember telling God, "But you were not there when my mother left me." His response was, "Yes I was." I asked, "Where were you when my mother rejected me?" He responded, "I was there." I said, "What! Where were you when she beat me?" He said, "Right there next to you." I asked, "Where were you when I was crying and lonely and hurt?" He said, "I was right there next to you. I was hurting there with you." I said, "That's not true. You were not there. I did not see you. Where were you when my mother was kicking me and beating me up with the rolling pin?" He said, "I was there I suffered the same things".

My response was, "You never suffered what I suffered. How could you be the one suffering? I was the one rejected! I was the one unloved! I was the one homeless." I reminded God how I slept in the barn with the sheep. He said, "So did I." I responded, with an attitude, "No you didn't." It seemed to me as if God was copying me, like He was saying whatever I went through, He went through also. But of course I didn't understand this. I had never read the Bible. I would later discover that He actually did go through these same experiences, even before me, so He knew exactly how it was. He knew exactly what I was feeling.

I asked him, "Where were you when my mother beat me over the head with a rolling pin, to where my ear felt like it was missing?" He said, "I was there." I then asked Him, "Why did you let her do that to me? Why did you not stop my mother?" He responded, "She did that on her own. I just protected you". I asked him," How?" He said, "Look at you. Your bones were not broken, you never had to go to the doctor." I did not understand what He was saying at all. I was not relating to Him having suffered like me or being lonely, rejected, beaten, or abandoned. I said, "How can I forgive my father, when I stood at that window day after day watching, waiting for him to come home, crying myself to sleep. He was the only one that I loved, yet he did not love me back." I then heard God say, "But I loved you." I could not understand this and I was feeling a little bit confused. How can this God, that I cannot see, love me? This was my argument, but I did not win, for Christ had forgiven me when I asked.

Finally, I came up with a plan. I would say the words with my mouth, so that this voice would leave me alone. I thought I would fool God. I would say I forgive them, but He would not know inside my heart. Inside my heart I would not forgive them. I would never forgive them. I could not forgive them. I knew that I could not, but again I thought I would fool God. Maybe He would leave me alone and stop prodding me to forgive. I remember saying the words out loud. One time I said, "Mother! I forgive you." I then heard the voice say, "Say it again." So I repeated the words again, "Mother! I forgive you." I was still thinking I would fool God. I had no intention of forgiving her, but I obeyed the voice, hoping it would leave me alone. I named all the things that I was going to forgive her of, but again I was only trying to fool God. I heard the voice again say, "Say it one more time."

For the third time I found myself saying the same words, "Mother! I forgive you." I named all those things again. When I was finished, without the voice telling me to say it again, I said it, but this time on my own. Tears were rolling down my face as I said, "Mother! I forgive you. I love you and I forgive you." Something was happening inside me. I actually was freely forgiving my mother now. They were not just words anymore. It was coming from inside, out of my stomach was flowing a forgiveness that I had no control over. I said it over and over and over; "Mother! I forgive you. Father! I forgive you. Ex-husband! I forgive you."

I started jumping. Praise took over. Inside me, and I began to say, "Lord! I really do forgive my mom." I said, "Oh my God, I really do, forgive her." I am now 43 years old, and for the first time in my life, I forgave my mother. I felt so relieved, so clean. I kept repeating over and over. "Oh my God, Oh my God, I forgive them." There was an explosion taking place inside of me. I'm free, I'm so free. I will never forget that day; the day I got free, simply by forgiving others.

I felt clean for the first time in my life, no fear. I was free from the darkness that had me bound all those years, and I could feel it. All my life I feared how I would survive, pay my bills and simply make it. Here I was all new inside, I felt a power I knew nothing about cleansing me of this dreaded fear and darkness. My hatred was gone and there was no one to blame anymore. I feel as if I loved everyone and 40 plus years of bondage were gone. It was the most wonderful feeling I had ever had. I didn't know what was next, but I have been washed, without soap and water, on the inside and it was great.

For the first time in my life I actually started to love myself. I belonged to God. Feeling this freedom I began to pray for my mother and father to be forgiven and saved as I was. I can see now that my heavenly father loves me, is on my side and caring for me. I was free from the poison of hatred and blaming others. Fear is gone. I'm special and I feel brand new. I can't explain it, but I know it's true. That same voice inside me, was telling me I needed to find a Church fellowship. I was driving down the road later that week and I saw a church beside the road that caught my attention. I said to myself, "There's a church. Maybe I should go there." But the voice inside said, "NO! Not there." I continued looking for a church, but I didn't know where to go, or where to look? I knew with all my being that I had to find a church

At the apartment where I lived, there was a community pool area, and I went to the pool. Lying on a table by the pool were books and magazines left there for people to read while they relaxed at the pool. I found a Bible among those books. I opened it up. There was no name inside, so I took the Bible; I thought it would look nice on my coffee table. I had often seen people put books on their tables, so I put this Bible there on my table. I did not read it. I just wanted to look good if somebody was to come to my house. I thought if I had a visitor they would see the Bible (unopened just lying there on my table), and I would look good. You might say I stole the Bible and put it on my coffee table, without the slightest knowledge that if I had read this book it would have changed my life. I just brought it into my home, as a good luck charm, the Word of God, without knowing what it could do if I had read it.

Don't, laugh! I was only a few days old in God. My son even asked me, "What is this book?" I explained that it was just a book that I found at the pool. "It had been there a long time and nobody else took it, so I thought it would look good on our coffee table," I said. "I'll take it back one day." I never thought I would return the book, but I just didn't want to tell my son I had stolen the Bible. I still have that Bible today, ten years later. I know what you're thinking and no, I did not end up stealing it. I saw a preacher at the pool one day and I asked him about the Bible. I told him I had <u>found</u> it at the pool and I asked if it was his. The preacher said," no, it was my sons, he left it there, but you're welcome to keep it if you want to read it. I had no intention of reading it, but I thanked him anyway and I kept it. I kept it right on top of my coffee table. It made the table look good!

My son was starting to have problems again, so I decided I needed to find a church to help him, and to help me with him. Deep down I knew the only solution was to find a church, but where? There seemed to be so many churches, but where would I go? I had no direction. How would I know whether it was a good church? One day as I was on my way to the grocery store, I accidentally took the wrong road. Passing over a bridge, I turned around and headed back in the right direction. As I was crossing in the middle of the bridge I looked off to the side and I saw a church. It was a very big church. You could not miss it. It had a beautiful cross on top which caught my eye. The small voice inside me, said, "Go to that church." It seemed as if I was on fire. I knew I had to go there. The following Sunday I attended this church and the first message I heard was this forgiveness stuff again. The preacher was telling us how free you become when you forgive others. He told us why Jesus died, and how He forgives us of our sins. I was sitting there thinking this preacher knows what I have gone through. I said to myself, "This has just happened to me. I must be back here next week. This is good; there's something here that I like".

After the service, many of the people came and greeted me, making me feel welcomed. Outside people were shaking the preacher's hand, so I went over to introduce myself. I don't know where the words came from, but I said, "Hello, I want to be baptized." Those words just came out of nowhere, because they were not my words. I didn't even know what baptism was. He said, "Okay, what is your name?" I told him my name and I was just standing there like a deer in headlights: I had just asked to be baptized, and I didn't even know what baptism was! His response was, "We will have to come to your house and talk to you, so you understand what baptism is." He set an appointment, and they came to my home that week.

I explained to my son that I had visited a new church, that I liked it very much, and that the preacher and somebody else were coming to visit. My son had been giving me some problems and I warned him, "If you embarrass me in front of these people, I will pack your bags and throw you out." He said okay and when they came to visit Nathan was on his best behavior. As a matter of fact, the preacher must have forgotten why he came. He and the other guest focused their attention immediately on my son. They were talking to him about getting saved. "Do you know Jesus?" they asked. He said," Well, I've heard about him." They asked him if he would like to accept Jesus; but he responded; "No, not at this time." My son glanced at me and I gave him that look that only a mother could give. They asked him again, and just to make me happy he said, "Yes." They prayed with him and another wave of God's peace came into my house. I had my stolen Bible sitting on the coffee table, so I guess; they assumed that I knew something about God. We discussed baptism and made the arrangements for the very next week. I was baptized along with seven others, me being the last one in the water. I was afraid to be the first; I wanted to watch the other people, as I had never seen this before. The preacher dunked me under the water and when he pulled me out there was this strong wind blowing across the baptismal pool. It was as if we were being blown down by the wind. The pastor remarked that he had not seen this before. My impression was let's do that again, it was awesome. It felt so good, and I had obeyed the word of God. I came out of that water feeling as if I had been energized with power. I would later find out that the Holy Spirit is often expressed as a wind that will come into an individual, filling their life with power.

Now I had an unusual desire to read the Bible that I had stolen from the pool. I saw that everybody in church was reading a Bible, so I would too. I started at the beginning of the Bible, but found I was not very interested in that part, especially when they get to the genealogies. So I skipped over them. The voice inside me was telling me, "Turn those pages back." I ended up in the Gospel of John. When I got there, the voice said, "Read this." I started reading there in the gospel of John. I could not believe what I was reading, and I was so amazed.

I was beginning to understand that somebody loved me; Jesus loves me. This book was obviously about that Love. I did not want to put it down. I thanked and praised God. I couldn't sleep at night. I just had this enormous desire to read more, more, and more. The more I read it, the more I understood. I could not comprehend this love. A love where a person would give their own son to pay the price for somebody else, who I perceive they did not even know. The more I read, the more I wanted to build a relationship with this God. Through reading His word, I was beginning to understand just how real God is, and that He wanted a relationship with me. He loves me. I am overwhelmed that somebody loved me!

Reading in the word I discovered that God wanted to be my Father. I thought to myself, WOW, I can have a father again. I also read that God said, "I will never leave you nor forsake you." This was great news to me, for my parents had forsaken me, but now God said He would not leave me. I found the verse in **Psalms 27:10** that said; **When my father and mother forsake me, then the Lord will take me up. (KJV)** This Scripture was a real blessing and comfort to me. Jesus had taken me up as His child. I was feeling loved, important, but I did not know why or how?

CHAPTER 12

A JOB FROM GOD

I began listening to Christian music and reading the word of God. I would watch as many TV preachers as I had time for. Often, I would call them for prayer as things arose in my life. I was growing in the knowledge of God. As time went on, I found myself being cut loose from things in the world that were dragging me down, or causing me to doubt. Sometimes these things would catch up to me and overwhelm me. I reached a point in my Christian life that I had to put my foot down and say that's enough. Then, I would declare, "God is going to help me! I am going to make it through! I belong to him! He's my Father! I can trust him."

One day while watching a TV preacher, He said to take a piece of paper, and write on that paper what you want God to do for you, and be specific. He said, "Tell God what you want, then place that paper in your Bible. Carry it with you wherever you go, pray over it, believe that God will do it, then sit back and wait on God to bring it to pass." That day, I wrote down on a piece of paper, Lord, I need $ 500 a week to pay my bills. I then named all my bills, writing each one of them down, along with my needs. I told Him I needed another car because the car I had was not running very well, so I wrote it down. I told God, "If you can keep my car running so it will get me to work, I don't need a new Mercedes. I just need a car to get me to work and take me to church. That will make me happy." I wrote it all down, placed it in my Bible, just like the preacher said, and I prayed over it daily. It was not very long before I lost my part-time job of cleaning, and then they cut my hours at the nursing home. I was in a reverse mode.

I had written the things down, I was going to church, I was reading the Bible, and I was giving to the church, five dollars a week.

I heard them talking about tithing, and I said to myself, I can barely give God this five dollars and he wants ten percent. I heard a voice telling me, 'God doesn't need your money. He already has enough, so you should keep your money," so I agreed with that voice. I convinced myself this was the right thing to do, especially since I was short on money anyway. My finances started getting worse and worse. I was praying for a new and better job.

Another evening as I was watching TV, I felt this voice inside me telling me to call the TV show. I called them, and don't you know I got right through. I told them I needed a job with at least five hundred dollars a week in pay. That preacher prayed with me right over the phone. I made a commitment that night that the first check I made from this new job, I would send it to his ministry as an offering to God. They did not ask for it, I just volunteered.

I heard about an agency that was hiring, so I went there and filled out an application. The owner who interviewed me rejected me right away. She said, "You have no experience; I cannot hire you." Something inside me took over. I know now it was the Holy Spirit. I said to her, "That's what you say; that's not what God says. My God says I can do all things through Christ who gives me the strength, and I will have the job with you. You will hire me".

I knew this agency was hiring people to work for multimillionaires, and she kept telling me that I did not have the quality or the experience. I did not meet the specifications for what she was looking. I went home and again prayed over my list that I was carrying in my Bible. In my mind I saw myself paying my bills, having a nice car, working a job, and everything going well. I called her a few days later, and asked again for a job. She responded, "I already told you, we don't hire people like you. You have no experience. I can't give you a job." I had more than enough experience as I worked in a nursing home for about four years. Again I told her, "That's what you say, but my God says you will give me a job." I kept calling her over and over for about a month, and each time she would turn me down. I was desperate. I believed God would give me the job, so I would not give up.

One day in desperation, I again told God about my need for a job, and how much money I needed. I also committed to pay a full tithe of my pay. I called the lady again at 9:15 in the morning, after my prayer. She told me not to call anymore and hung up on me. At 11:15 the same day, my phone rang and I could tell by the caller identification that it was the agency calling me back. Now I was very nervous. I was almost afraid to answer the phone. Deep inside I know this was it. My hands were shaking as I answer the phone. It was the lady from the agency, and she said, "Radica, I have a job for you. It pays six hundred and fifty dollars a week. Its five days a week. Monday through Friday." I wanted to shout, but I simply said, "Yes, yes!" I asked when I could start this job and she responded, "They want you to start at six o'clock today. Can you be there?" "Absolutely, I'll be there," I answered. She gave me the address, and told me she would check with me before six o'clock to make sure I would be on time. She called back in 15 minutes with another job offer. This one would pay a little more money and she added, "With this other job, you won't even have to work nights, just days." I told her, "I'll take that job," thinking it is more money, which has to be better.

I don't know exactly how it happened. I drove to what was supposed to be the second job, but by mistake I ended up at the address of the first job, that she had told me about the one with less pay. I called her to let her know I had arrived at the job, and when I told her where I was, she said, "You went to the wrong job".

I was in West Palm Beach, Florida, standing in front of the client's door, apparently at the wrong job, but I rang the bell. My heart was just pounding. I didn't know whether I would be accepted or sent back to the agency. Ms. Levi came to the door wearing a pink sweater and black pants. What a coincidence, I was wearing the same thing. She was shocked that I was wearing the same colors. I later would find out that pink was her favorite color. I looked at her and noticed she had blue eyes and blond hair just like me. She took me into the residence and I sat on the couch. I looked around at the room. It was the penthouse of a high-rise condominium.

I had just met the elderly woman that I was going to be taking care of. She was a beautiful, sweet, elderly Jewish lady. She looked at me, and the first thing she said was, "My God, I'm going to keep you, you're so pretty." I did not know at the time that this lady had fired everybody who came to work for her, usually within a day or two. The agency had sent many people there, and they never lasted very long. The agency gave me the choice to go to the other job that would pay more money or stay with this lady. I decided staying was the thing to do. I felt something inside telling me to stay with her. The agency then told me, not to get too comfortable or unpack. It won't last long: three-day tops, because she hadn't kept anybody.

I was questioning God, wondering why she did not keep employees. I was being drawn to her, wanting to keep this job, and reject the other job offer. I heard this voice again, saying, "Look at her. She's lonely, and she needs somebody to love her. All she needs is love." I respond, "Oh God, Wow! I can do that." That night we had a long conversation before she went to bed. I asked if I could give her a hug. I probably was not supposed to do that on the job, but I really liked her. I worked for this lady five days a week and someone else would come in on the weekends to take my place. My job was simply to sit with her and cook for her. I was hired to stay with her 24 hours a day through the week. I drove her to the doctor, to the supermarket, and wherever she wanted to go. I was being paid to just be there with her as a companion, so she would not be alone. Mr. Levi had passed away some time prior to this. Her children lived in another state, and she did not want to stay alone.

After working for two weeks, I went home for the weekend. Ms. Levi called to see if I had made it home okay. She called several times that weekend, asking if I was okay. When I returned to work on Monday, she said she was going to let the other lady go and just keep me 24 hours a day, seven days a week. She said, "I will go home with you on the weekends and stay with you, if that is ok." We did this some of the time, which was surprising to me, because she was very rich, and I lived in a very small apartment. She did not seem to mind where I lived, she just wanted to be with me, and she just wanted me close by.

I later found out that she would take me as a daughter, and that she would love me as a daughter. A few years later she let me know that she had a desire, that she wanted to die in my arms. "Not now," she said, "but when the time comes." She wanted me to be with her until the end of life. She asked me to commit myself to take care of her until the end. I'm sure this must have amazed her entire family. They had not been able to find anybody to stay with her, because she would always fire them.

Several weeks later Ms. Levi informed me that she traveled to New Jersey, and it was possible that she might move there. She asked if I would be willing to go with her to New Jersey. I told her that I would go wherever I was needed; it was part of the job. Ms. Levi did in fact move to New Jersey to be close to her family. She had her life wrapped up in her family, her children, her grandchildren, and great-grandchildren. Ms. Levi was very proud of her family. Until her very last day she remembered all their names. Even when the Alzheimer's was taking her memory, she still called each of them by name.

After working for her some time I met her family; especially her son "The Doctor." She would always say this is my son, "The Doctor." I had talked to him every week on the phone, but now I was going to meet him face-to-face. We went to his house in New Jersey. I had never seen such a beautiful home. Dr. Levi and his wife greeted me as they were coming out of the garage. We went inside, I met the whole family, and we had lunch together. After lunch Ms. Levi told her son, in my presence, I want you to accept Radica as family. He came across the room, and gave me a big hug, along with his wife and his children who also accepted me. Over the years we developed a very strong relationship, as a brother and sister. Even to this day he calls me sister. If something happens to me and I forget to call him or don't want to bother him, he scolds me just like a brother would. Although his mother is gone we still have a family relationship. He still calls me often and we talk, just as if we have been family forever.

Ms. Levi liked to read and kept her eyes on the news. She liked to keep up with current events. She often wrote letters and recipes. One day while reading, she asked me what book I was reading; I told her it was a Bible, and she asked if I would read some to her. She also asked me if I went to church, even asking if she could go along. It just happened, the very Sunday she went to church with me the message was about blessing the Jewish people. Ms. Levi was shocked, yet surprised, she questioned whether they knew she was Jewish. She thought maybe; that was why they were talking about blessing Israel. She had a good time and wanted to go back from time to time. When the church found out that she was Jewish, they welcomed her gladly, calling her the Jewish princes of the church. This made Ms. Levi excessively happy. She loved to be complimented, and did not hesitate to compliment others. If she liked you, you would know it.

I was thrilled to know how much Ms. Levi loved me and prayed for me. She said she was praying for my peace, happiness, and for a good husband. Today, I can say God answered that prayer of hers. She was always good to me, loving and full of life. She liked to travel anywhere, as long as she could shop when she got there. She was over-protective of me, even getting jealous of anyone I talked to. She was worried they were trying to hire me away from her. She always cautioned me she would no longer be my mom if I talked to others. I told her more than once she was like a jealous husband, and she would say she wanted me to only love her. I assured her my heart was to care for her as long as she lived.

Ms. Levi was proud of me and did not hesitate to show how much she loved me as a daughter. I wondered how the family might have felt about her openly speaking about her feelings. Ms. Levi would often come into my room after I retired to bed and crawl into my bed rubbing my hair and saying how proud she was of me. I remember I had wished my own mother had done this same thing. I would remember how I crawled into my mother's bed that first night and the feeling it created in me. How I had longed inside for this same feeling, until now. Ms. Levi would cover me up and tuck me in. I had to raise my bed up high so Ms. Levi would not be able to get into it, for she thought she had to be motherly over me. She was over ninety years old and would explain her actions as doing what good mothers do. I reminded her I was not a child and she would say yes, I was her child. If she only knew how much she was fulfilling a desire of my heart since I was four years old. She often wanted to talk all night long, but I needed sleep so I could take care of her.

While attending church one Sunday we had a missionary from South Africa visit. He told me, God was going to send me back to my country, and there God was going to show my family and friends that He is God. He said that God had taken hold of my life and that He had blessed me. He went on, "God is going to bless you young lady, so that those who see you will be jealous of God's blessing in your life." Then God spoke to me through him saying, "You will go home to be a witness to your family and your country. Everyone will know that I am your God, and that I have done this for you."

During the last months of Ms. Levi's life, it was clear things were coming to an end. I would not have enough time to tell her how much I loved her, and how much she had blessed me. To this day I sometimes think I hear her voice. We planted roses together and each time they bloom, it is my reminder of the time I had with her and how attached we became. She would smell the roses, reminding me this was her favorite color, pink. This would always bring me back to that first day I met her wearing that pink sweater.

Until the day Ms. Levi passed away, she never forgot my name. There was never a day that she did not know who I was. Even on her deathbed she called me by my name. The last words I heard Ms. Levi say, was about the love she had for her family and me. I comforted Ms. Levi, telling her she would soon be shopping in heaven. I told her the malls would be open 24/7 and she would be the number one shopper. She had a sense of humor, right up until her last day.

I can say that being in her family changed my life. It felt as if we were blood relatives. I learned so much from them, but most of all, I experienced the love of a family. The missing link in my life had been found. I now have a brother and sister-in-law I love dearly, and I fit in. It would be quite some time before the family would find out things in my past, as I was not comfortable talking about these things. Even now, when they read this book, it might surprise them to learn some of the things that I went through before I knew them, and some of what has happened in my life since our meeting, especially the love of Dr. Levi and his wife. They made me feel so comfortable. I have been so loved by them that if I had not gone home to visit my family in Serbia, I probably would have forgotten a lot of my past, or stuffed it away in a secret place instead of reaching the forgiveness that made me whole. I could never thank the Levi family enough for the love that they gave me, nor how they took care of me while I was taking care of their mother.

A few years after I started taking care of Ms. Levi, I started calling her mom, because she insisted she truly was as mother to me. Ms. Levi developed Alzheimer's and dementia. The job would demand more of my time, more stress, and of course more patience. But the love that God had shown to me by placing me with this family helped to equip me for the task at hand. I was able to love this woman by lovingly taking care of her. I washed her, fed her, and poured my life into her final years. It was later that I would discover she was asking God to provide a husband for me. She knew that she would be going home, and she wanted me to get married before she left. This is another story of my life, another chapter, another challenge, another blessing. She told her son "the doctor," that she would not leave; she would not go until she knew that I would be taken care of by a husband. She was the first woman to take that motherly position and show that motherly love in my life. I shall never forget it, although sometimes I thought she was strangling me, showing too much love. Sometime I would get overwhelmed, never had I experienced people being this kind.

I later found out through reading the word of God, that God had made a promise I knew nothing about. My husband got to speak at her funeral, his first Jewish funeral. At the funeral he shared a Scripture about the blessing of Abraham (**Genesis 12:3 And I will bless them that bless thee, and curse him that curseth thee: and in thee shall all families of the earth be blessed. (KJV)** I can truly say, my life has been enriched and blessed beyond measure because I took care of this woman, a Jewish woman, a descendent of Abraham, for more than five years. I was taking care of her, a descendent in the line of Christ Jesus, and Christ was taking care of me, fulfilling the promise to Abraham. I thought of this many times during the last year of her life.

I cannot share with you all the benefits and blessings I received from the Levi family, for it is private and the family might not want it known. However, while I took care of Ms. Levi, her son Dr. Levi raised my pay during that five-year period of time as the job demanded more from me. The family provided my transportation, a brand-new Mercedes-Benz. They paid the insurance, and gas, what a blessing they have been. Upon her going home, they gave the car to my husband. He was shocked. He only spent the last 16 months with her, but they respected him. Dr. Levi would often come to our house, visiting his mother, and he would see how my husband helped to care for her needs. My husband took care of Ms. Levi the same way he would want someone to care for his own mother.

The Levi family showed me how to love, how to receive love, and how to reach out to other people. Ms. Levi taught me patience, family, love, and I think she even gave me my sense of humor. Being with Ms. Levi taught me how to laugh and enjoy life. She gave my life worth and value. I pray God's blessing on the Levi family daily for all they taught me.

CHAPTER 13

REMEMBERING THE VISION

It had been a long time since I had the vision that first week of November 1975, and now it was 2005. Thirty years had passed and so much had happened. My life had certainly taken on new meaning and purpose these last 5 years. I have seen God at work in and through me and I'm excited at his marvelous deeds. I remember during one of my days off my daughter Savanah and I were spending the day together. We had gone for some coffee. It was raining and because of the rain, we decided to sit in the car. Savanah was moving around and because my car was new, I asked her to sit still and not spill her coffee. Savanah then said she did not like her name and she wanted to know who had chosen her name. I explained how she had been named after her grandmother. She went on to ask about Simon, and as I was explaining about Simons name I saw a flash in my mind of the uniform he wears as a policeman. She then asked about Angela, explaining how she really wanted to know. I said she was named after her great-grandmother. Savanah asked about Nathan. She wanted to know why I would name my children after those terrible people. I explained that I thought her father would love them if they had his family's names. Suddenly, the whole vision came back as if I was having it all over again.

As I remembered the vision; I started crying, which startled her. I then shared my vision with Savanah as I remembered it. She asked, "What kind of a God would let a person go through all this hurt and abuse?" I said, "My God, and one day you will find Him too." She responded, "Never." My prayer as a mother was that she would see the change in me and come to know My God as I do. One Sunday Savanah, Angela, and one of their friends showed up at my church. I think they wanted to check it out and see where I was attending. While they were checking my church and I out, Christ checked them out. We went home to change our clothes. The girls were sitting on my bed, and asked how I had made such a change in my life. It was obvious to them something had transformed my life, but what? Both my daughters stated that I was not the mother they had grown up with, and they wished I had changed back then. The joy and peace I had was so obvious both girls believed their lives would have been different, better, if I had changed when they were young. I explained that I did not do it, I could not do it, but Jesus could and He did. I asked them if they would like to receive Jesus and make a change. Right there in my room, on my bed, I led all three girls to salvation. Hallelujah!

CHAPTER 14

TRYING TO RECONNECT

Having truly forgiven those who wronged me, I was being guided by the Spirit inside to contact my mother and my father to tell them that I have forgiven them. At this point I did not know where my mother lived, and I did not know how to contact her. I remembered the town's name, but not the address. I had no idea whether she still lived in the same place, for she often traveled to other countries. I went to the church, and I asked the church if they would pray for me, and ask God to guide and direct me on how to find my mother and father. Most importantly I asked them to pray for confirmation that God truly was directing me to do this. The church prayed for me, and within a few days I had a dream. In my dream I was awakened, and told to write down an address. The first address that I wrote down was my father's address. The second address that I was told to write down was my mother's. I told the church about this dream, and that I had sent letters to these addresses. They were praying those addresses were the correct addresses, and again they were asking for confirmation that this dream was from God.

Two weeks later I received a telegram that said my mother was still alive. Yes, she did live at this address, and attached was a phone number for me to contact her. Oh my, now I didn't know what I would do. I had the number and couldn't decide whether I even wanted to call. I decided to write a letter instead of calling. In this letter I explained to my mother how good God had been to me, and how He had protected me all throughout my life, even though I was unaware of His protection. I told her how He had brought me to the place where I was now, peaceful and forgiving. I told her my health was good and that I was doing well. I even thanked my mother for giving me life, and I told her I forgave her, for the choices she had made in my life. I ended it by saying that I would love to actually see her face-to-face. I told her I loved her and again thanked her for being my mother. I received a letter from her stating that she had received my letter and thought that I had to be either nuts or on drugs, to even think that she would need to know about this Jesus that I had found. She was embarrassed because I had become a Christian. In my country Christians don't talk about being Christians. She said she was not interested in meeting me. She had her own reasons. I accepted the letter with lots of reservations in my mind. I was hurt but decided it would be best to just leave the situation alone. My job was finished; I had peace in my heart. I knew that I had done the right thing. If my mother would die now, she would at least know I forgave her, and I had told her I loved her. No matter what would happen now, I was at peace. This was important to me.

I sent a letter to my father as well, with the same basic message. I shared with him how God had been good to me. I had a feeling in my heart that my father probably was not going to live very much longer. I don't know why I had this feeling, but none the less I did, and I could not shake it. It is because of this feeling I felt it necessary to use this opportunity to tell him how he needed to accept Jesus Christ, as I had done. In my letter, I told my father that I forgave him for the past, and that if he ever needed me as a daughter, I would be there. I went on to write, "You're still my daddy, and I love you. No matter what had happened, it's forgiven."

I never heard back from my father. I didn't know if he had even received the letter, so I sent a second letter thinking maybe my step mom had not given him the first letter. Still, nothing. I heard no response. I did not have the same peace that I had inside after hearing from my mother. There was this feeling of urgency I could not explain away. I just had to get in touch with him. Somehow, I just felt that he needed my help. I sent my daughter, who still lives in Serbia, a message asking her to see if she could find my father, her grandfather, and check on his well-being. I gave her the address I had sent the letters to and sent her money so she could travel to where he was living. She informed me that she had gone to see him, and my feeling was right. He was very sick. He was in need of help. I sent my daughter the money to buy him the things that he needed. I was going to take care of him, somehow, even though I could not go to Serbia. At that time I did not have the proper papers to leave the USA.

My father informed my daughter that he had no intention of connecting with me. He didn't want to deal with it. He said he was not interested. My father knew that he was close to dying, yet he rejected that one last chance that we could have had together. He had cancer, so I paid people to stay with him, to watch him, and to check up on him often. My daughter was now involved and checking on him. Anytime he had a need she would tell me, and I would send money to help. A few months passed and my daughter received a phone call saying that my father had passed away. It was Thanksgiving Day, 2006. I could not go to my father's funeral, for my passport had expired, and I could not get it renewed in time, so I sent money to help with the burial.

I gave my father a good burial even though I was not able to attend. While making the preparations my daughter found my letter in his pocket, the last one I had written. He must have carried it with him in the same way I carried the wrapper of the candy bar which he gave me when I was seven. Perhaps it was his way of holding me one more time. My daughter informed me that the letter had been found, so I knew my father had received it. I will never know why he didn't communicate back; maybe he was ashamed, perhaps he was overwhelmed with guilt, or maybe it was just like always, he just didn't care. Since he is gone, I don't know the reason, and may never have the answer. I will leave it in God's hands.

My heart still hurts today when I think I never had the chance to hug my father, to kiss his face, to tell him I loved him, face-to-face; but that was his choice. Oh how I wish I could have felt my father's hands around me one more time, just to hear the words, I love you. After realizing my father was gone, I began to experience the emptiness of being alone. I had deep grief as you can imagine. I kept telling myself that I knew my father loved me. I knew my father did care, but the emptiness was consuming me. I kept telling myself he loved me, because I did not want to deal with the possibility that he did not. I would remember that long bicycle ride, his tears falling on my head, and those words, "I love you."

I think it was at this empty time in my life that I began thinking about what it would be like to have a good marriage, to have a good husband to be there with me. I wanted someone to share my life with. Someone to fill up some of the loneliness I was experiencing as I was missing my father. Maybe I wanted to share my pain with somebody. I am convinced that I needed somebody to come into my life at this time.

I focused some of my attention while praying, asking God for a husband. I prayed and I believed that He would do this. I was still taking care of Ms. Levi at the time, and she also was praying that I might find a man suitable for marriage. She said she was praying for me to find a husband, and she even said that she would not rest in peace if she did not find one for me. She was a beautiful woman, very attractive, even in her old age. She was over ninety and concerned that I needed a good man. She would remind me, from time to time, that before she could pass away she would have to know that I had found a good man. She would have to approve of the marriage, and she would have to be responsible for training him to be a good husband, just like any good mother would.

She obviously had a wonderful marriage herself. Her husband had provided very well for her, and she wanted the same thing for me, for she considered me to be her daughter. She would often tell me of the love and wonderful times she had with her husband, and their travels around the world, and she was going to find somebody like that for me. She would say, "I'm not going to die, unless I find you a good man, if I can't find you a good man, I'll just have to take you with me. Firm in her belief, Ms. Levi was in every way treating me as a daughter, even though I had been hired by the family to work for her. Her love easily passed as my mother's love. She even called herself my mommy. She refused to let me call her Ms. Levi. She said, "You've got to call me mom." So I named her Cookie. Every time I would turn around, she would try to take cookies from the jar. She loved cookies. "Cookie" would remind me often that a mother is one who gives loving care to a child, not necessarily the one who gives them life.

CHAPTER 15

MY HUSBAND

I began seeking God more often, specifically for a husband. But I would always remind him, if you have a husband for me Lord, bring him to me and let me know he's the one, but if not Lord, I'll be satisfied with you. I had been in church for a while, and I had heard several messages on tithing, so I was giving God ten percent of my income just as I had promised before I got this job. I was expecting nothing in return. I was doing what most people I assume do in church, I was paying the tithe to help keep the church going. But in my heart I was thinking I was doing My God a favor with my tithe and expecting nothing back. This was my way of thanking him for saving me.

I was sitting in church one Sunday, when the lady sitting next to me said to me, "Radica, have you considered giving God a tithe for a husband?" This sounded ridiculous to me, so I laughed, I thought she was joking. I had been giving to God expecting nothing. Now she challenged me to give to God expecting something from my giving, and of all things-a husband. I thought this is too weird. I would later find out, and it would be emphasized to me by my husband, that giving to God expecting nothing, is exactly what you get. My husband would teach me, if you plant a garden, you do not put the seed in the ground, and then spend time watering and fertilizing it expecting nothing in return. He would explain, "We don't give to God just to receive, but we do plant seed in God's kingdom, expecting a harvest.

The next time I came to church, I was thinking about what the lady and told me. When I put my check in the offering, I wrote across the bottom. "This is my tithe LORD, for a husband." Actually I put an "H" so no one would think I was crazy if they saw my check. I put my money in the offering, chuckling, believing in my heart that God would do the same, laugh at this.

Several months passed, and my birthday was coming. Ms. Levi, took me out for dinner with my friend, we were in New Jersey at the time. We were to meet at the restaurant at five o'clock. I always drove Ms. Levi wherever we went. Along the way we were stopped at a red light a block from the restaurant. I had my hand on the steering wheel and I looked down and I could see a wedding band on my finger. It was shining as if the sun was flickering off of it. I reached down with my other hand to try to touch it, and then I realized, of course, I didn't have a ring on. At this time I did not wear any rings. I didn't like things on my fingers, so I just didn't wear them. I passed it off as one of those things, it wasn't really happening, "my imagination" I thought. I proceeded on to the restaurant. As we were sitting there, I shared it with my friend, just for laughs. She just started laughing at me. After dinner we went back home. I was in the living room, reaching for the remote control for the TV, when I saw it again. I was looking at my hand, and I saw a ring on it, glistening from the light. But there was no actual ring on my finger.

The next day was Sunday so I went to church. I told my preacher about the ring, and how it appeared on my finger. I said to him, "Look, I don't drink, so I wasn't drunk. I'm not on any medication, so it's not drugs. I don't think I'm crazy, but this will sound crazy to you." I told him what I had seen. He just smiled at me and started laughing. I said, "Hey, it was my birthday. What does this mean?" He responded, "God is showing you, one of two things. (1) God might be saying you're married to him. (That's it; I thought) (2) Maybe God is saying he has a husband for you and that you will be married someday." When my preacher said "husband" to me, there was a peace that came over me that was so filling that I knew this was from God. His truth for my life. From that day on I began to thank God and praise him for my future husband. I increased my giving to God, and wrote a letter, telling him what I wanted in a husband.

I wrote to God that if he had a husband for me, these were my demands: I did not want a man that does not love God as I loved God, one who puts God first, somebody who has the same peace and joy that I have in God. One who will serve God along with me throughout our lives, plus a few other things that I wanted. I told the Lord that he would have to reveal to me who the man would be, but in a very special way, so that

I would not make a mistake. I did not trust myself in these matters. I had made enough mistakes in my life, and I didn't want to do that again. This time I was willing to wait on God, whatever he had in store. I had a great fear I might choose the wrong man, and I told God about it. I was afraid I might fall in love with the wrong man, and ruin my life, and especially my walk with Him.

In the past I had paid attention to my fleshly heart, and I thought if I followed my heart I would make good choices, but I was wrong. I know now, that God says my heart is deceitful, and above all things, desperately wicked. I do not know my own heart. I reminded God of the Scripture saying don't let me follow my heart, let me follow your heart. The husband that you have picked out, bring him to me, and don't let me fall for anybody else. From that point on, I began to pray for my future husband and his family.

It would be more than a year before I would see things start to take place, to fulfill the prayer that I had prayed for a husband. In the meantime, Ms. Levi and I moved back to Florida because she could not take the cold of New Jersey. I was attending a church and enjoying the worship one Sunday. As the worship service was going on, the spirit of God was so strong it felt as if everyone was worshiping God. My worship was interrupted and I felt a small voice saying to me, "Look on your right side." Prior to hearing this voice, there was a lady standing next to me during the service. As I looked to my right, the woman was standing there still worshiping God. The voice said, "Look over your shoulder." As I looked, I saw a man standing there. The voice said, "Look at his face." I was thinking to myself, why would I want to look at his face, I'm worshiping Jesus. I want to be in the presence of God. I'm not concerned about someone else in the church. This happened three times. After the worship service had ended, we sat down. The preacher began to preach the message of the day. I looked around again and there was no man there, I looked behind me and to both sides just to make sure I wasn't seeing things, I even asked the lady next to me," Did you see that man in a blue shirt standing between us?" She replied, "There was no man there." After the service and during the next few weeks, I would tell a few people in the church about the man that I had seen, but none of them seemed to know of that person. For some reason I was stirred up. No matter what I did, I couldn't get this experience out of my mind.

Because of this incident, I started going to God with more specifics. I laid out before him some specific things I wanted Him to do, if indeed He was bringing somebody to me to be in my life. I did not want to be fooled.

I would need a few things to happen so that I would know the person that He was bringing into my life was from Him. A few short days passed and my son and daughter came down from New York to visit me. They signed me up to a Christian internet dating service. I objected, and they answered me, "Mom, do you see men banging on your door? Do you see men lining up for dates? Do you see men waiting to take you to dinner?" The answer of course was no. They explained to me that this was a Christian website and that it would be safe.

Everyone this website matched me up with, I had no interest in. Finally, the people who run the web-site called me on the phone and wanted to know what was wrong with all the people they had matched me with. They even wondered if there was a reason why I did not contact them. I simply told them that when I saw the person I was waiting for, I would know who and would then make contact. My son kept telling me, "Mom, they're Christians. The website is for Christian's, so what's your problem?" I just wasn't interested in spending time looking at people on the Internet. I was waiting on God. Sometime during the next 30 days a name came to me, "Tim," and the number 53. I shared this information with my son Nathan.

My 30 day membership had expired, and I was happy. My two children would be happy, because they felt like they had tried, and it was all over with no one catching my attention. I was quite okay with that. Finally, I received an urgent message from a match named "Tim." I told my son that my membership was over and that I should not be getting any more matches. I thought this site is just trying to get me to sign up for a longer membership. My son started to read the profile. He stopped and reminded me that I had told him about the name Tim and the number 53. He said, "Mom you will not believe this. This man's name is **Tim and he is 53** years old." With this, I decided I would take a look. As I looked at his page, I remarked, "I know him from somewhere." I saw on his profile, that he was a preacher so I thought maybe I saw him in church somewhere. I would soon realize I had seen him in church, but not because he was actually there. He was the man that I saw standing behind me and the other lady in the church during the worship service some time earlier; howbeit he never was actually in that building. Now I was a little fearful, I have to wait on God, step-by-step, waiting for the things that I had asked God to show me, if this was the man from Him.

Tim did not live in Florida any longer, although he had lived here earlier. He had moved to Alabama. He was in town because he was getting ready to go to Haiti on a missionary trip, I would later find out. He was in the library, paying his bills online, when the message popped up on the computer, *we have a match for you*. He sent me a message saying that he was only in town for three days, on his way to Haiti, and that he lived in Alabama. They were not supposed to match us up because of the distance. We were five hundred thirty miles apart. He also added his phone number, to which I responded I don't call men, and gave him my number. He called and we made arrangements to meet the next day.

The next day came, but Tim had decided to go to a revival in Lakeland, Florida, instead of meeting me. I was fasting during this time, and seeking God's direction, yet at the same time I was excited because I had recognized Tim from the picture as the man standing behind me. The next day Tim did not call me, I assured myself that God was going to do this. My faith in Him was strong and I trusted Him to work out all things in my life, yet at the same time I knew this was the person for me.

I shared my excitement with Ms. Levi and asked for her advice, as she was excessively smart and full of good advice. She said, "Well, Radica, if it is meant to be it will be. I have to see the man you're talking about. I don't want just anyone to marry my daughter." (Now I had to be careful to listen to her for she was not easy to please, and was very protective of me.) In my nervousness, I asked her how she would know if he was good for me. She said, "Oh I will know. Trust God to do the right thing."

I asked her permission to meet Tim for coffee, out of respect for her. She responded, "Oh yes! I think **we** should **both** go meet him." I called Tim and asked if he would be willing to date two women at the same time, explaining how Ms. Levi wanted to see who I was meeting, and had no intention of letting me go by myself. I was caring for her day and night at this time and was not so sure that she might want to run Tim off; and she would if she did not approve of him. The first time she met Tim she made an instant connection, and liked him immediately.

Tim did not know it at the time, but I certainly did, that God often spoke to me in dreams and visions. So when I have a dream, I begin to ask God immediately what it means. This is a prophecy of Joel Chapter 2, "when the Spirit is poured out on flesh, people would see dreams and visions." I did not ask for this, it just became a part of my life. Tim did not call me the second day, so I just left things in the hands of God. The evening of the second day I had a dream and I saw a cloud in the sky, and upon the cloud was written "God with you." I said to myself, "I know that God is with me, but what does this mean." I had a second dream and again it was written, "God with you." I heard a voice say, "Look to your right." I looked and Tim was standing there, smiling. I saw the cloud again, "God with you." After the third time, I asked God to tell me plainly what the dream meant. I realized it could have been just my own mind playing tricks, because I had been thinking about Tim. I was made aware by that small voice that God was telling me, "this is the person" and "I am with you. I will work it out." I must say again, I did not trust myself. I had to wait on God and know He was leading me. I would not trust my heart, because when I did this in the past it turned out to be a disaster and a disappointment.

On the third day, no call all day, but around 3:30 in the afternoon Tim called. He said that he had been waiting, but God had put it in his heart to call. He went on to explain that he was busy and really didn't want to call until after he came back from Haiti. He told me he was on his way back to St. Lucie County and that God told him to call me now, so he obeyed; but he was going to wait until he came back from Haiti to meet me. When I talked to him on the phone, I told him about the vision that I saw with the clouds and the writing, and about him standing there beside me. He asked me to describe the clothes he wore in the dream. As I described the clothes, he told me that was exactly what he was wearing right at that very moment.

Now, I had his attention. I had just described exactly what he was wearing. Tim told me, I have to have dinner with my children tonight before going to Haiti, and I will not be finished until about seven. I explained to him that I was not interested in meeting him for supper because I was fasting, which I did on a weekly basis. We made arrangements to meet after seven o'clock, when he would be finished with his children. He said we would not have a lot of time because he had to get ready for Haiti.

We met at a restaurant in St. Lucie West for coffee. We sat and talked until the restaurant was ready to close, about 10 o'clock. For the first time in my life, I told this man, whom I didn't even know, my whole life story. For some reason I just had this urge. I knew I had to tell him everything, even the things that I was ashamed of. I heard a voice saying, "Do not tell him those things, he will leave." But the still small voice inside said, "Tell the truth, tell him everything." I thought to myself that if I told him everything he would run and never look back. He's a preacher, I was sure he would think I was crazy. Who tells all about themselves on the first date? He probably never experienced this kind of crazy stuff, of this I was sure.

I told him about my vision, the one I've outlined in this book. He just sat there across the table and never blinked. He just kept staring at me. I could not tell whether he was listening from his heart, or if he just wanted to run. I remember I was so excited explaining my vision, and how I got saved. I don't think I gave him much time to talk. I had to get this out; something was pushing me to tell my life story to this man. I had no idea why this was happening. I can assure you, I would never tell anyone on my own. Some of the stuff, as far as I was concerned, was too embarrassing and nobody should ever have to know that God had forgiven me of such things. Further, I did not really want to talk about it, feel it, and think about it. The Holy Spirit was having me say these things, especially since it was the first time I met this man.

When I was finished telling him my story, he said he had a few questions. I did not know at the time, but I would find out later, he was listening to my story about the vision, trying to figure out if there was one thing that did not agree with Scripture. He shared this with me after he came back from Haiti. He first asked me to tell him how big Satan was. I looked at him, puzzled, wondering, of all the things I said, why, would he ask me how tall Satan was. I told him, in my vision; he was a very short man about three and half or maybe four feet high. He just laughed. I did not know at the time, that the Bible indicates Satan was small, and the world would look at him and laugh, saying that's the man who caused all the trouble in the world. Tim was very much aware, that the Bible said this about Satan. He shared with me later in our relationship, how many people describe Satan, and most of them think he's much bigger than he is. I didn't know what the Bible said; I only knew what I saw in the vision. I checked it out later, and I found that he was right. Satan is very small; he actually is only as big as we make him.

He also asked me whether the Angels I saw were men or women, for again, as a preacher he knew there are no female Angels in the Bible. But I did not know this; I never had a reason to question about Angels. My answer was simply, in my vision they were young men, all of them about thirty to thirty five years of age. I explained, this is what I saw in the vision. All I know is what I saw.

Tim told me that night, while we were at the table, that my vision matched the biblical descriptions and he was interested in my story. After hours of talking we got ready to leave. I could not tell by his expression what he might be thinking; it seemed as if I might have puzzled him. I had no idea what part might have startled or taken him by surprise, but

I knew I had told him exactly what happened in my life. I told the truth, and I was excited. I thought to myself, that if he got in the car and drove away and never called again, that would be fine.

We walked out of the restaurant to the car, and I was still talking. They may have closed up the restaurant, but I wasn't finished. He told me he had a couple CD's of sermons that he had preached, and asked if I would like to listen to them? Giving them to me, we said our goodbyes. He had to go to Fort Lauderdale for a trip to Haiti, and I was going home. I was about to leave, when he turned around and said to wait, he had something for me. I took a deep breath. I said, "Oh, Lord, this is one of the things I put before you. Whoever God had for me, he would have to give me something with red and white in it. Three times red, for the blood of Jesus, and three times white, for purity. This was something between me and God alone. I ask God for this sign so that I would know that he was the man from God. I also had told God, that the man He had for me must quote me a Scripture.

He handed me a box that obviously was jewelry. I did not even look at it, I just placed it on the seat beside me as he quoted me the Scripture, saying, "If you are the person I am to marry, I will love you as Christ loved the church. We then went our separate ways. I did not look into the box. I was afraid to in case it wasn't red and white. I did not really want to know at the moment. If this was the right person: and in my heart I knew it was, I was too nervous to take a chance. Upon arriving home, my son asked me; if I liked him? I said, he was nice, a Christian, loved God, and he serves God. I was very happy. I went to the bedroom, and waited for him to call. He told me he would call to make sure I made it home safely.

Again, a little voice told me to open the box. My first response was to open it the next day. Two hours passed, but no call, I thought, He probably won't call. I didn't understand because everything seemed okay. Everything seemed to be falling into place just the way I had asked God. I thought, here it is; he said he would call, but he did not call. I heard it again, open the box and look at it; just look at it. Reluctantly I opened the box. I started yelling with excitement, I was red and white, red and white, red and white, just like I had asked God. White diamond and red ruby, earrings! As I was looking at these earrings the phone rang, It was him, he told me he was sorry he didn't call right away, but he needed a little bit of time to sort out all the things that I talked about. He was also questioning God; because he did not want to make a mistake in his life either. We discussed how we would correspond when he came home from

Haiti, among other things, as I recall. When we hung up the phone I began a fast for his work and safety in Haiti.

When he arrived back in the states we began communicating by phone for a short period of time. It would become apparent to us that God was in the middle of our lives, and we were each seeking God's direction and will. My future husband was getting ready to do a revival in Pennsylvania and I wanted to see how God was using him and how he handled ministry, so I flew up on my days off. He picked me up at the airport with his mother and brother. We saw a great move of God in this revival. The Lord was using both of us as his vessels, and people were just amazed how easily we flowed together in ministering to the church. Some time through the meeting someone sent a note to the pastor to read to the congregation. **Psalm 85:10-13 Mercy and truth are met together; righteousness and peace have kissed each other. [11] Truth shall spring out of the earth; and righteousness shall look down from heaven. [12] Yea, the Lord shall give that which is good; and our land shall yield her increase. [13] Righteousness shall go before him; and shall set us in the way of his steps. KJV** They knew my husband well, and were excited at what God was doing for him. It was a confirmation of our relationship being of God. Upon hearing this scripture the whole church was in tears and the pastor could hardly read it.

The power of God was present to heal and deliver. Many secrets were revealed by the Holy Spirit. Tim's mother was concerned that I might not be able to submit to his leadership as a husband and as a man of God. She would express her concern, while telling Tim how much she loved me already. This would not be a problem for me, as I was asking God for someone to lead me into a closer walk with Him. I wanted a husband who could make decisions and take authority as the Head of the house.

Tim soon proposed to me and I, of course, accepted the proposal. Tim had already asked my son and Ms. Levi for permission to ask me to marry him. Ms. Levi was thrilled and acting very happy that day, as I recall. I questioned her about the thing she and my son seemed to be hiding from me. She simply said my prayer is answered. I assumed her son was to visit as she was always excited when he would come. Later that day she told me I should dress up, as Tim was coming over. When he arrived he was holding a large bouquet of roses. He came in and sat next to Ms. Levi on the couch. As I entered the room; he got on his knee and asked me to marry him. I started laughing at him, telling him to get up, adding that Ms. Levi was not going to accept anyone in my life at this point. Tim then told me how he already had her blessing and acceptance. I accepted the ring and ran out to the room where Ms. Levi was waiting to hear my answer. She grabbed me and we cried together for joy. After a few moments she wanted to know if Tim had a place for her in his house, as she was not going to let me just go off with him.

Tim and I agreed that we might have to wait until Ms Levi passed away for the wedding to take place. I would fulfill my commitment to her. We agreed that unless her family approved of her living with both of us, this is what we would do. I informed Dr. Levi of my being engaged. He was delighted to find out I had found someone. It would not be long until he came to meet Tim, and approved of the marriage, agreeing to let his mother stay with us after the wedding. We were soon to be married at a small chapel in Stuart, Florida. A minister, and friend of my husband, agreed to do our ceremony. Of course, attending the wedding was Ms. Levi, and she was proud and happy to be a part of this change in my life. Ms. Levi blessed our wedding, and after a short honeymoon we settled into our lives together.

I remember the excitement of everyone who heard our story of how we met and came together. We were blessed with the attendance of his children and mine, each expressing their love and acceptance of us. The grandchildren were also present and part of the wedding. One of them asked me if I was going to make their grandpa happy, saying he deserved to be happy. I truly love them all and to me, they are all our children.

One of the events that has taken place in my marriage had to do with my passport. My passport was about to expire because Yugoslavia is no longer a country. My country had changed its name to Serbia. All passports had been deemed invalid after one year. My husband's family does a lot of traveling, two or three trips a year, and most of the trips involved traveling abroad. I decided to become a US citizen, and Tim helped. I made application for US citizenship. Everything had changed since 9/11 and the attack on the Twin Towers. I studied and studied for this citizenship test. Day after day I went online, and took the test. There were one hundred questions on it. Each day I would miss only two or three every time.

The day came for me to take my citizenship test. My husband drove me down to the immigration office, which was an hour drive from our home. On the way, he asked me all the questions on the test. I again missed one or two but that was okay, you didn't have to get them all correct. I was aware that during the test I would probably only be asked 20 of the 100 questions, this is how it works. Something happened that I cannot explain. I certainly did not like it; it was confusing, and yet it happened.

My time came to go into the office. A young lady came out and got me, and we entered her office. She began asking me questions about my children, about their births, and other things that I should have known. On any other day the answers would have come immediately. I knew when my children were born, I knew their names, but in that office I could not remember my own children's names. I could not remember their birth order, or the days they were born. I could not believe this was happening to me. I feel stupid and confused. I studied for months for this test. I knew all the correct answers and I couldn't remember anything. I couldn't remember who the governor of the state in which I lived was. I knew these answers, but the answers were not coming out. The examiner even gave me several chances to give her the right answers, but I just couldn't answer. I couldn't remember.

I left the office and she told me they would notify me of the results by mail, in a few weeks. As my husband drove me home, I just sat there speechless. He asked me several times how it went. I did not know how to tell him that I could not answer the questions. I was feeling ridiculously foolish, but I could not remember my children's names in that office. I did not know, nor could I believe, that this was an act of God. God was getting ready to open up to me and my husband a word of prophecy that had been spoken over eight years earlier in my life. It had been prophesied that I would go home to my country and there they would see the work and power of God in my life. My family would see his blessing on me and even be jealous of his blessings in my life.

CHAPTER 16

GOING HOME 2009

I had been married now for a year and a half and Ms. Levi had passed away, leading me to start a new chapter in my life. My job taking care of Ms. Levi had kept me from traveling with my husband, for she took all my time, but now I was free to travel to Haiti with him and help in the mission work. To see firsthand what God was doing in Haiti.

During this time I felt like I should go home to my country of Serbia. The feeling was stronger while I was in Haiti. I wanted to take my husband to meet my family, especially my daughter. We were intending to go to Serbia simply as a vacation. While in Serbia I would also have to apply for my Serbian passport. We purchased tickets for a two week trip. I was going home to my country, I was sure God was with me on this trip and I asked God to let me see my mother while I was in Serbia. I asked God to work on my mother, so she would accept me, and acknowledge me, and love me. I heard Him say, "She will not accept you. Don't build up your hopes." I said, "Yes; I believe she probably will, when she sees that I have peace and joy." I went on to explain to God the story of Luke 15, how the prodigal son went home. I then went a step further and even told God what I would say, and how I would speak to her. But God said, "She will hurt you again." I was not afraid of this, I knew I could run back to God's arms because of his love. I told God I just wanted my mother to hug and kiss me for the first time in my life. I just wanted my mom to hug and kiss me, while she's still living. I then reminded God, "You are able to do anything. You can change her. You can make her accept me."

My mother knew we were coming; my daughter had informed her that we had arrived. My mother told my daughter, "Yes, I would like to see her." We had booked the cheapest airplane tickets available, but when we got to the gate to board the plane, the flight attendants took our boarding passes and told us to step aside. This was during the time when security was high because of terrorism. I asked my husband, "What did you do?" We were assuming we were in trouble. They were not smiling at us, and it seemed as if we were being pulled aside as an example. To our surprise one of the top officials of the airline arrived at the counter, and the flight attendant says, "This is them." Now I figure we, for sure, had done something wrong, because we had a discussion with the flight attendant about our carry-on cases. They wanted to charge us more money and we refused. The official responded, "Okay; these are the ones," and then he smiled. A few moments later they handed us first-class seating. Everyone else had already boarded the plane, and here they were moving us up to the first-class section. I said to my husband, "Look at this. My father, God, is sending me first-class to meet my mom. This must be a good sign."

While in Serbia renewing my passport, I would need to prove my birth and residence as a child. I had to visit the city record's department in the city where I was born. My daughter had gone there on my behalf a few times, and they could not find any record of my birth. The night before I went to the record's office, I had a short vision. In the vision I saw an older gray-headed man finding my records. As we drove there I told my husband and daughter what I had seen. My daughter informed me the only person she saw there was a young man, and she had been there more than once. When we arrived at the office the record keeper was a young dark haired man. I enquired if there was an older man who worked there. He said he was the only one for record's, adding he had worked there quite some time. He looked for some time and could not find me in the books. In Serbia, records are all hand written in volumes of books, and my name was not there for the year I was born.

I was getting a little nervous because I needed this information for my passport. He was looking and talking when I heard someone in another room coming in. He was an older man, gray-headed and he had been listening to our conversation. When he asked who I was he entered the room where we were. He proceeded to tell me his grandmother and my grandmother were sisters. He had worked in the office many years before. He knew where my record was. It was in book number--- and page number---. It had been over twenty-five years since he put any records in the books, yet he then went to the exact book and said, "I wrote your name and information here on this page. Your mother refused to register your birth." He also added, "Your father also did not register you. Now, I remember your Father, came in to register you when he wanted to send you to America. I remember I wrote it here for him." That day I found out I actually was a year younger than I had been told.

He made a copy of the page for me and I went to an attorney to have it made into legal papers. Attorneys are expensive and hard to get an appointment with in Serbia, but he saw me with only a ten minute wait. Upon hearing my story and knowing exactly what I needed, he instructed his secretary to give me everything I needed, before anyone else. One hour later I was leaving that office with all the legal papers. He also refused to let me pay him for the work. He said he just could not believe any parent could refuse to register their own child. He blessed me, and sent me on my way. The government would have had to make a search of all states in Serbia to see if any hospital reported my birth and this might have taken several months. In less than a month all the records were found and my citizen number was assigned. I then was able to proceed on to receiving my passport.

The next day after our arrival, my mother called me. I was shocked yet happy. We were in Serbia for about three days before we went to visit her. I had to finish my passport papers before I took on any visiting. I was very nervous about going to see my mother. I did not know what to expect, and I did not know how I would react. It was probably the longest ride I had taken since that day daddy rode me to her house on his bicycle. Driving down the road leading to her house, all the memories of my childhood came back. I could see the school where I had attended, and streets where I had slept many nights. We passed the bus station, and the train station, and all the different places that I would call "home" as a child. The emotion inside of me was overwhelming. I even questioned myself if this was the right thing to do. Did I really want to see her again?

We arrived at my mother's house, and pulled in the driveway. I was sitting in the back seat of the car along with my daughter. My son-in-law was driving, and my husband was in the seat in front of me. I had dressed up with the fanciest clothes I owned. I was going to make sure my mother saw me as a beautiful child. I wanted her to see me as I saw myself looking into those store windows as an abandoned child. I was wearing jewelry, and I had made myself up, just for my mother. As we arrived I saw my mother looking in my direction, just trying to see me. As I exited the car, my stepfather grabbed me and started hugging me. He started crying and said, "Look at you. Is this really you? You look just like a doll." he told me. At that moment I saw my mother and she was crying. As she came nearer, she hugged me and kissed me. She just kept holding me and crying. I think my mother had forgotten that other people were there. She took me by the hand and started leading me into her house. I was thinking; this is what I wanted her to do when I was just a little child, when Grandma brought me here. Here I am fifty-one years old, and my mother, for the first time, is holding my hand, leading me into her house. She kept looking into my eyes, astonished, telling me how beautiful I was. If I had only heard those words forty seven years earlier, how different my life might have been, I thought.

My heart was pounding because I could not believe this was actually happening to me. This was exactly what I had asked God for. Here it was happening to me. I did not know how to handle it. I was not as prepared for this as I thought I was. My mother was actually serving me coffee, juices, and water. It seemed as if she was not able to give me enough because she kept asking me, "Would you like something else. Are you cold?" On this day, my mother offered me her very own sweater. If she had only done this when I was a child, I thought. I was taken to this room, where my mother had made a feast. She had a large table spread in my honor and she had invited some of her friends to come over to the house to meet her daughter. The table was spread with every kind of food that you can imagine; desserts, breads, meats, salads. So much food, I could not describe it. My mother set me at the head of the table, where she could watch me and she sat there right next to me. She was holding my hand and making sure that I ate. The emotion at that table was too much, lots of tears and lots of joy. I looked across the table into my husband's eyes, and I could see that he was crying. He couldn't believe that she was treating me like this. We had discussed what we thought might happen, and agreed we were ready for anything.

After we ate, we sat there talking for quite some time. I told my mother I wanted to ask her some questions. She said it would be okay. I wanted to give her an easy way out, and so I said to her, "Mother, I would like to ask you about some things that happened to me. You can tell me, you don't remember, and that would be fine. Or you can tell me, that is true. Or you can say, Radica that's a lie, and that did not happen." I promised my mother that either way she responded, it would be okay, I just had to ask. She asked if she could ask me a question first. I agreed. She said, "How was it, that all the things you said as a child, the things you would do, you have been able to do them all? How did you know as a child what you would do?" She added, "It troubles me very much, to know that the things you said as a child, are what you are living today. You said you would get on a big airplane and leave this country, and you did. You said that you would have peace, joy and love, someday, and it's obvious you do. You said you would be rich. You obviously look rich." I did not answer, but instead I asked her, "Why did you leave me? What was the reason?" She said, "It was because of your father." I remember telling her, "I don't blame you. He was not a good provider; he was an alcoholic." This might not make sense to you as you read this, because it does not make sense to me. I said, "Mom, "why, didn't you take me with you, when you left my dad? Why did you leave me?"

My mother looked straight into my eyes, and said, "When I was bringing you home from the hospital, a large snake crossed the road in front of us. Upon seeing the snake, I knew at that moment you were not supposed to be with me." I asked my mom, "Why, did the snake tell you to leave me?" I was making light of this because I thought my mother might be joking. In my country people are superstitious and practice witchcraft, although they don't call it that. "I could not take care of you," she said, "because of the snake," I was waiting for my mother to say I'm sorry for leaving you, but the words never came. As far she was concerned, the snake was her excuse and all she needed to believe to justify herself.

I asked her why I was not allowed to sleep in the house and why she rejected me after my grandmother brought me back home. Her answer was simply, "I couldn't, I just couldn't." She then said, "I have to confess something. I always cursed you, for you to die. I even cursed the plane that you would fly on, when you went to America. I told her that I was aware that she had done that. She asked me to forgive her for cursing me, and I said; "Mom I forgive you, for everything." Her response was, "What!" Then she acted as if she didn't have the foggiest clue what I was talking about. In her mind she had done nothing wrong. I guess it was that snake.

My mother then went on to tell me that it was because of her that I am what I have become today. I could not sit there and let my mother take the glory. I said, "No mother, you're absolutely wrong. I am what I am today because of God. He had me in His hands from the day you gave birth to me and left me. I have always been in His hands." He made me what I am today." Since my mother did not believe in God, she was shocked. I was sure she must have thought, "How could you be in God's hands?" to her there is no God.

My mother acknowledged that all the things that I had said about my childhood were true, even in front of her guests and her friends. She would later explain to her friends, after we left the country, that, "My daughter put a spell on me while she was here, and I had to lie. I don't know how she did it, but she had a spell on me, and I could not defend myself while in her presence." My mother wanted to show me all of her wealth, and she has a lot of things. We started going from one house to the other and from one room to the other. It was absolutely shocking that my mother had the same decorations, same bedspreads, same taste in design, as I had in America. My husband would say to me in each room, you have the same kind of glasses, dishes, bedspreads; even the pillow settings are placed on the beds the same way. This was unbelievable. It was as if the same person had decorated both houses. I was shocked, and said to myself; "Oh my God, I'm just like my mother. Oh God, forgive me," I said. "I don't want to be like my mother."

My mother then paraded me through the town, as if she had something to brag about, I was her pride and joy that day. As we went from business to business and from home to home, mother holding my hand, telling everybody, everywhere, this is my daughter, you would've thought that my mother raised me, and was the greatest mother in the world. She paraded me into town; people were looking at me funny. It was obvious they had this puzzled look. Why would she do this, they had to be thinking. They all knew she had abandoned me. People's faces would light up, and I would hear them say, as they recognized me, "Thank God." I even heard them say, "Oh there has to be a God, look at her". One of the store owners said to me, "Oh my God, you used to beat me up. We were in the same class." I asked him, "Why would I do that?" He said, "Because we were teasing you because of the way you were dressed. You were always dirty, we made fun of you, and you would get mad and beat us up."

I saw an elderly couple looking at me and he's had a camera, taking my picture. "We must show this to everybody," he said. "Nobody will believe this." My mother was proud of this. She is not getting it. My mother seemed clueless that these people were saying these things, not as a compliment, but rather as, I can't believe this woman is pretending to love this child after the way we saw her treat her as a child. Some people even questioned her about her soul. One family that knew my mother and had lived next door to us knew how I was raised. They were both at a very old age, hardly able to walk, but they came out to me when they recognized me, and began to hug me, crying and saying to me, "Is it really you?" After several minutes of love and sharing with them, my mother, stood there bragging about me to these people. They said to her, "Aren't you afraid of God? You didn't help her get to this place in life." My mother simply replied, "Afraid for what?"

The lady asking my mother this question was the same lady I mentioned earlier who had taken care of me when I had sores, from the barn some forty years earlier. She started crying, calling out to other people saying, "Look, there is a God, Yes! There is a God." (Fulfilling the prophetic word spoken over me back in New Jersey). "Do you know who this is?" she would tell them. "This is the shepherd girl that I told you about many years ago," she said. She called her husband who at this time was disabled. He could hardly walk, but he came all the way to the gate. Looking into my face he also started praising God. He said to me several times, "Is that really you? Look at you. Is that really you?" These two people had helped me during my childhood, by giving me clothing, medicine for my sores, and the old man had actually fed me many times. The couple then turned to my mother, and said," There is a God, look at her; just look at her! You are going to pay for what you have done to this child."

The couple stood there telling me this, and my mother stood there beaming, taking the glory as if she had done something great for me. These people were touching my face, kissing me, and rubbing their hands in my hair, taking pictures of me, and pictures of me with them. Many of the people from the town were coming outside because they had heard that I was in town. In my country news spreads very fast. It's a small town and everybody wanted to know what had happened to me. That day I received more praise, more "Oh wow's," more "Oh my God, is this really you, more reactions from people than I had ever received in my life.

We stayed at my mother's house late that night and as I was talking to my mother, we were leaning on each other. It was as if we had never been apart. My mother even asked me to spend the night in her house. Somewhere in our conversation I looked into my mother's eyes. I could see deep inside. "This is you, God, at work, not my mother." I heard his voice, "Yes, it's I. You asked me to do this and I did this for you." I remembered a verse that came to my mind: **Psalms: 23:5 Thou preparest a table before me in the presence of mine enemies: thou anointest my head with oil; my cup runneth over**. (KJV) I looked at the table still spread with food, and then I looked at my mother. I looked across the room to where my husband was sitting, and said, "I'm ready to go." My mother kept asking me to stay longer, but once God revealed to me it was only His work, I was ready to go. I needed to get away from here, and I wanted to be by myself and just cry.

We got in the car that night. We had been there about nine hours. As we backed out of the driveway and headed down the road, I looked back at my mother through the window. As I waved good bye, I saw my mother as the woman she was before, the same look was in her eyes from my childhood. It was scary as I now remember what God had said, "She's not going to accept you. Don't get your hopes too high; it's not going to happen." As we were driving home, I was very emotional. I could feel God's arms around me, and my daughter was also holding me, trying to comfort me. My daughter had tried several times to build a friendship with her grandmother, and she was rejected each and every time, so she was very uncomfortable just being there. I could feel God's love in the car, it was all around me. I could almost hear him saying, "I told you this would happen, but you wanted to meet her."

I said in a small prayer, "God, I thank you. Now I know what it feels like for my mother to hug me, to call me beautiful. Because of you, my mother, even though it was for only a few hours, was proud of me." I knew in my heart it was God at work, for my mother would not keep this opinion of me. I pray daily for my mother's salvation, lest she should end up in the pit I saw in the vision.

A few days later, my mother drove to my daughter's house unannounced, just to see me. My mother was hugging me, and kissing me, but it did not feel the same as it did on that first day. We sat and talked for a few hours, when the purpose of her visit was exposed. My mother said, "Radica, I need your help. I need to talk to you about something." My mother then told me she had a terrible fall-out with my half-sister. The law had been involved for about a year or two, and they were fighting things out in the courts. My mother had thrown my sister out of the house, with nothing, and without money. And now my mother was trying to keep my sister from receiving anything from her. My sister and her husband had slaved for my mother their entire adult lives, with little or no pay. They were entitled to some of my mother's possessions and money, and my mother wanted me to go to court with her and lie for her. She wanted me to say all her possessions were actually mine. She asked me to tell the courts that I had given her all her wealth. She wanted to cheat my sister and her husband out of their rightful compensation. My mother is a wealthy woman with great possessions: land, tractors, animals, and houses. My mother had used anyone and everyone, and used any means necessary to obtain this wealth.

My mother's only pride and joy in life were her possessions. She had always had to have more than anyone else, and her possessions had to be bigger than everyone's. My mother tried to convince me, that she had rejected my children because she was forced to do so. She told me my sister was so jealous of me that she had threatened to leave the house and move out, if she accepted me or my children. This of course was not true, for she had rejected me long before my sister was born, but that was my mother's excuse and her way of trying to keep me and my sister angry and apart for her own benefit.

It was being impressed upon me while my mother was speaking that my sister, whom she held out to me as an infant saying, "This is my child," was now being rejected, by the same mother who had rejected me. Now my mother was pretending to accept me, and rejecting her daughter. The one she so boasted to me about. My little half-sister. **(Matthew 19:30 But many that are first shall be last; and the last shall be first**. (KJV) While listening to my mother. I' was thinking of this Scripture,

My mother continued to try to explain to me the reason she needed me to lie. She then confessed that she had already informed the courts that all her possessions belonged to me. She did this because she thought that I had become a US citizen, for I had lived in the US for some 35 years. In Serbia, US citizens cannot inherit family wealth, you must be a Serbian citizen. So my mother lied to the courts about her wealth saying that I had given it to her and that it all belonged to me, this way she was thinking that she could escape giving anything to my sister, who is a citizen of Serbia, and I would never be able to inherit, because she thought I was a US citizen. It was sad yet funny when I thought about it. Here was a woman that all my life rejected me, but now was ready to accept me as her daughter if I would help her to save her wealth. I told my mother I would not lie, and she simply got up and left.

My mother was unaware that I had made contact with my sister prior to her arrival, and that my sister and I had long conversations about our childhood. I wanted to know if my sister remembered my rejection, and how I was treated as a child. She remembered most of it, and even told me things that I had forgotten. She explained to me how she wanted to play with me and have me as her sister, but our mother refused to let her. I could

119

tell by listening to her that she had hurts in her life as deep as mine. Even as a child she could not understand why things were as they were.

Tim and I spent another week with my daughter and her family. We were then to return to the USA. The day after we left Serbia, my mother went to the tractor store and purchased a brand-new tractor, telling the family she could prove I bought it for her if it came up in the courts. She said she would be able to prove I was in the country, and therefore bought it at this time, and this would prove to the courts that I had bought her all her possessions. My mother had someone drive the tractor hours out of the way, just to show it to the family. It was her new toy, her new possession. It was not enough for my mother to just buy something. No, it had to be bigger, and better than anybody else's. My mother had inquired diligently about what my husband and I owned. My husband had told her he had bought a tractor. It just happened to be bigger than hers, but he did not tell her it was thirty years old. Thus, she had to buy this new tractor so she would have a bigger one than my husband's.

After I returned to the US my sister contacted the courts. While my mother had told the courts a lie, that I had bought her all this stuff, my sister was one step ahead of her. My sister told the courts about me. She told them I was her older sister. The judge put a stop to the whole case. He asked my mother if it was true that she had an older daughter. My mother had to say yes. My sister informed the court that she had abandoned me and had not taken care of me. The court told my mother and my sister that the first child has the rights of inheritance. All this is now a matter of court records. My mother saying everything belongs to me, and my sister confirming I was not cared for. Both of them were informing the courts for their own reasons. My mother for the purpose of keeping all her things and cheating my sister. She also thought I was a US citizen and in a sense cheating me. My sister informed the court to show that our mother was heartless. I see God working do you? I could care less about inheriting anything from my mother, but God might have other plans. Whatever God wants will be for His glory.

CHAPTER 17

GOD USES MY TESTIMONY

Six months later, we would return again to visit my daughter and her family. This trip would be different, for our intention was not just to visit. We were going to share Jesus with as many people as we could. Serbia was a communist nation until 2000. They have some churches, mostly Orthodox. It was very plain to see, on our first trip, the people did not know much about God. It was plain to see religion was in many places, but when you would talk to the people, their knowledge about Jesus Christ and what He has made available to us through His death on the cross was almost nonexistent. On this trip, I would discover how desperately spiritually poor the country was.

I should first say that my daughter had accepted Christ Jesus, several years earlier. She had been communicating with me, and we had many discussions during our first visit privately. This trip was to be about a month long. I would be celebrating my birthday in my home country. On the way there, my husband and I agreed in our prayers that God would send us to those whose hearts were open to the gospel truth and keep our eyes and minds closed to anyone or anything that was not going to benefit His kingdom. On our first trip we only shared the Gospel with my daughter and her husband. She was already serving God, and although life is hard in Serbia, she was growing in Jesus daily. She was into the Bible and had much knowledge of who Jesus is and what was expected from Christians to serve their God faithfully.

On this trip we would venture into the open market, where I had seen the vendor who I spoke of on the first trip. I was drawn to her booth and was instructed by the Holy Spirit to purchase things she was selling. We began a conversation and she poured out her life and heart to me. She asked if she could come to the house to discuss Jesus and the peace I had with Him. She was told by God that I had answers that would help her, as I was leaving the market on our trip six months earlier. We set a time and she came with some friends to hear the gospel.

We led her and her friends to Jesus. While on this trip we would see 24 others come to Christ through her, Cora. She would bring them to me to hear my testimony. She would be what we would call "our woman at the well that Jesus met." Her changed countenance and lifestyle would influence many more to come to Jesus for salvation. During this trip, we went out late at night to baptize Cora and her daughter. We drove quite a distance to a warm mineral spring, coming up out of the ground. It was a little cold outside, but the water was warm at this spring so it was there that we were baptizing. There were many other people in the water, who were watching us, as this is a place where people go to swim and to soak in the mineral water. I was standing on the bank as my husband baptized Cora and her daughter. I was standing next to Cora's husband and her son, and we were watching the baptism. It was a perfectly calm night. There was no cold wind, everything is going beautifully and Tim started to baptize Cora. As my husband was putting Cora under the water, a very strong wind started circling around. Upon watching the trees swaying in this wind, people started looking at each other. Cora's husband had a shocked look on his face and asked, "Where is this wind coming from?" When Tim finished the baptisms, upon coming out of the water, immediately the wind stopped. I remember the Scripture where it says the Holy Spirit came as a rushing wind. **Acts 2:2 And suddenly there came a sound from heaven as of a rushing mighty wind, and it filled all the house where they were sitting.** (KJV)

This is also what happened when I was baptized in America. There was a wind that was present upon my leaving the water, and even the preacher noticed it. This was our first baptismal service in Serbia, and Cora's husband was so impressed that he declared he wanted to be baptized also, but at a later time.

I asked my husband, when he came out of the water, what he thought about the wind that started blowing and he responded, "What wind?" I explained to him about the wind that we were feeling up on the land and he looked around and laughed. He didn't feel anything. He was busy baptizing, so his mind was on the people!

One day we were invited to a home in Petrovic. A mother there lived with her son, who was possessed. It seems, as she told it, when he went outside his brain would tell him day is night and fear would overtake him. He attacked anyone he saw with the intent to do them harm. Once while under attack, the mother told us, her son took all the pictures she worshiped and prayed to off the walls of her home and tore them up. He then attacked her and was trying to kill her when the police came and put him in a mental hospital. He was now at home again, so we went to visit her son at the house. He told us, "A very strong and husky man appears with a lamp that was super bright in one hand, and a holy book (Bible) in the other, and reads it to him at night." Then this man says to him, "You will be ok, just wait, help is coming from America." As we began to share with him about Jesus he became very excited and kept telling us that the man in the hospital had already read that to him. It seemed that everything we said to him he had already heard in the mental hospital, but without understanding. Right there and then he finally understood all that we told him and all he had been hearing from the husky man, and he was happy to accept Jesus. He volunteered to accept Jesus, so we knelt on the floor in the room to lead him in prayer. In this same room was a forty-two year old woman who had been listening, and she too accepted Jesus. As we prayed and cast out the devil, this son started quoting scriptures to his mother and telling her about Jesus. It seemed the only one not truly open to the truth was the mother. The next day we received a message. His mother could not believe that her son woke up quoting the bible, calm, and happy for the first time in three years. The word was spreading through town about this boy, since everyone knew him and of his condition.

Another day, at the market, a woman was telling me how terrible her life was and how very bad she had it. As I shared my testimony with her, God was opening her heart and right out in the open market she received Jesus. Instantly before our eyes her face changed; her entire appearance changed. It changed so much others were coming around just to see what had happened. Some of them were pointing to her saying, "Look at you, you're totally different."

That evening we were invited to another home where a twelve year old boy had been unable to walk since three years of age. As I shared my testimony, the whole family received Christ, for they had heard of my past and now saw me face to face. The young boy told us in his heart he knew he would walk someday, but his father was very skeptical. He said, "I will have to see first." He had spent an excessive amount of money on cures and even witchcraft, even sending his child to monasteries where they claimed healings took place. God gave a word to Tim about this man's daughter, the problem she had, has been an embarrassment to her for all her life. God said, "Tomorrow morning, you will see, the problem will be healed. The father agreed to wait until morning. About 10 A.M. we received a phone call saying he now believed and now had faith to trust god for his son, for his daughter was healed that night. We heard from the family many months later and the daughter never had the problem again.

At 6:30 pm one evening two young ladies were coming to visit, to hear my testimony, but they arrived late. They brought along a friend, so all three were invited in. While I was sharing, one of the young ladies was doing all she could to keep from crying in front of her friends, obviously out of conviction. God said to me, "She is going to make a decision that will not only affect her, but her two friends. They are waiting for her to yes, first!" She seemed to be the leader of the three. When asked if they would like to accept Jesus they all said, "Yes!" After praying for salvation, we prayed for the left hand of the one young lady that seemed to be in charge. She had lost the use of her left hand some time back. Her hand was black, like the color of dark clouds. I was praying and expecting her hand to be healed immediately. My husband took her hand as the Spirit said to him "hold her hand and tell her about the man with the withered the hand in the Bible." As he obeyed the Spirit and the story was being told, he got to the part of the story where Jesus said, "Stretch out your hand." Immediately her hand started opening. She was shaking and moving her fingers and thumb. Her hand became so hot that it was dripping water onto mine. She was definitely expecting and believing for a complete recovery. All three young ladies agree to come back for a Bible study on how to pray, overcome fear, and abide in Jesus.

We were also invited to a lady's home who was a single mother; a school teacher involved with a married man (common here in the Serbia, a nation without God). The woman that was saved at the market had told her about the peace she experienced and she wanted to hear my testimony. As I was talking to her the Spirit told me to tell her about the woman at the well and her meeting Jesus, to tell about her search for peace with men and relationships, until Jesus gave her living water. She responded with, "That's me." I told her that was why God had me share it, and I asked her if she wanted that in her life. She was very educated and was weighing everything out, but in the end accepted Jesus. Her question was "Will I feel it?" The woman that took us there got this big smile and almost laughed saying,

"Oh yes, you will feel it." After praying, her face was happy and you could see there was hope in her eyes for the first time in her life. She admitted she knew her life was as sinful as it could be, up until that day.

Another woman came to see us about her daughter who was about fourteen. Since childhood she would wake up at night and terrorize the home by breaking everything and screaming in terror all night. The father had to sleep next to her to keep her from cutting and killing herself. He said he had not had a good night's sleep in over ten years. It was not immediate, but after several hours of sharing the gospel and my testimony she agreed to accept Christ. After praying with the girl, she was smiling for the first time in years. Later we were invited to their home and the Spirit revealed to my husband how she kept her arms covered so no one would see the scars where she had cut herself. When Tim told her he knew of her scars, she was immediately set free, and to this day she has been completely free and the whole family is rejoicing.

While we were there in Serbia, my daughter planned a birthday party, inviting several friends and of course my sister. My sister arrived early and said she would have to leave early as well. We had dinner together and were about to cut the cake when Cora, our first convert began to share how God was changing her life, giving her a peace she had never had. Cora had only been saved about two and a half weeks, but everyone she knew was making remarks about the physical and mental changes they saw. Someone interrupted, changing the subject and my sister said to him, "I'm sorry but I want to hear what Cora is saying." This was my sign. I looked at my husband and he was ready. When Cora was finished, my sister was crying and her husband was trying to hide his own tears. Tim asked them both if they would like to receive Jesus into their lives. That day my sister and her husband both became Christians. They were so focused on Cora and what she was telling them, they forgot to eat their cake. My brother-in-law told us how he had found a Bible in the home where he worked, and had read several parts of it often, but now he understood it was truth. They asked us why we did not tell them the first time we came to Serbia. We explained how God had directed us to just become friends the first trip and wait until He opened their hearts. This was their time; they were ready. When the time came to fly home they took us to the airport. On our way, I learned how God kept them awake several nights reading the Bible. They were so excited at what God was showing them from His Word.

I could go on and on about how God has used my testimony for his glory. But I'm sure it has touched you in some way. I'm glad to share my dark past if it will shed light to the readers and encourage you to also share your testimony. We all have one, and as my husband often preaches, "Your deepest secret is the very thing God wants to use to minister to others." There are many sitting in your Church, living in your neighborhood, and working next to you every day, that have been crushed by their past and could benefit from the testimony of Jesus in you. Let the Holy Spirit lead and guide you to share your testimony and see how God will use it to open doors for you.

I have seen God open doors to share my testimony, or just a few words of it, in stores to other customers and employees as they ring up my sales. Anywhere I go; I listen and wait on the Spirit to open hearts. I have led many to Christ in the market place, as I daily meet and see the hurt in others eyes, and can relate to them because of my life.

GOD USES MY TESTIMONY IN HAITI

I t was in Haiti that I would discover the great value of all I suffered as a child and as an adult. There the purpose of my life would be clearly seen. I was on my first missionary trip with my husband. He had been doing work in Haiti for years. He took me to remote areas of the country to minister to the women. Here I would find myself surrounded with hundreds of ladies who were victims of abuse. In Haiti it is common practice to abuse women. I shared my testimony and was able to reach their hearts immediately. They were shocked to hear that I had been through the same things they faced daily. I could see My God reach into their hearts, reveal the secrets, and expose sin. And we would pray for them. I witnessed firsthand the power of my testimony.

I spent several days surrounded by many children who were just as I with little or nothing to eat, due to poverty or abandonment. My heart broke as I remembered my past. Most of the children had only old clothes or some had no clothes at all. My past was being lived out in front of me. I spent days hugging and kissing each and every child, remembering how I wanted a hug and kiss from my mother as a child. I also would remind each and every child how beautiful they were.

A few women had serious issues with forgiveness. One morning I shared with them in our Bible study, of my having to forgive my mother and father. One lady asked me in a very angry voice, "Do you really forgive your mother? I will never forgive the woman I worked for. She killed my daughter and all my animals. I will go to hell before I forgive," she replied. She walked out of the meeting, but she did not go far. As conviction hit her, she bent over a fence rail, and I placed my arms around her and helped her to forgive them. Again the Holy Spirit was using my testimony to reach this woman.

I encountered several young women pregnant and unmarried, and again I was ready to minister for I had been pregnant and single, and raised my children as a single parent most of their lives. I again saw my testimony reaching them with hope and love. Each time I go to Haiti these young girls come to see me, knowing I can relate to them, for I have been where they are.

It is amazing to see how God has the right people prepared for the challenges of those He is calling to salvation and change. I am so excited to see how God is using my testimony, and although at times it is hurtful, I will gladly share it for His glory. When others see how I was truly IN MY FATHERS HANDS, they will see He also has them in His hands.

CLOSING PRAYER

I f you don't have a relationship with God through Jesus Christ, pray this prayer from your heart:

Dear Lord, I come to you in Jesus name. I ask that you will reveal yourself to me, so I may know you in a personal way. I acknowledge my life is a mess and I need help. If you are real, show me and I will surrender and obey you. I am open to you now and want to have an intimate relationship with a true and living God. I repent of my sin and accept you, Jesus, as my Savior and Lord. I believe you died for my sin and rose again on the third day. I believe you will reveal yourself to me and change my life. I thank you Jesus for saving me.

If you are a child of God but haven't shared your testimony pray this prayer from your heart:

Heavenly Father, I come to you in Jesus Name. I first ask you to forgive me for not sharing with others what you have done in my life. Help me, Lord, to become bold to share with others how you have changed my life. Remove the embarrassment of my past and let me use the testimony of my past as your tool to minister to others. Give me boldness to lead someone else to you through my witness, and to encourage those around me to receive and share their testimony for your Glory. Help me to listen for the Holy Spirit to open the door to share. Give me patience to hear others, equip me with an answer from your Word that will help them and use me for your glory and purpose, because I belong to you. I have authority over fear and doubt and intimidation. I will not be defeated by my past, instead I will use it to destroy the works of Satan in other's lives. Amen.

Romans 10:9-11

That if thou shalt confess with thy mouth the Lord Jesus, and shalt believe in thine heart that God hath raised him from the dead, thou shalt be saved. [10] For with the heart man believeth unto righteousness; and with the mouth confession is made unto salvation. [11] For the scripture saith, Whosoever believeth on him shall not be ashamed.

Romans 10:13-15

For whosoever shall call upon the name of the Lord shall be saved. [14] How then shall they call on him in whom they have not believed? and how shall they believe in him of whom they have not heard? and how shall they hear without a preacher? [15] And how shall they preach, except they be sent? as it is written, How beautiful are the feet of them that preach the gospel of peace, and bring glad tidings of good things!

CHAPTER 19

REFLECTIONS FROM MY LIFE

Chapter 1   My Childhood

The things I spoke as a child came to past in my life. I said I would become rich, fly away from Serbia, and have nice clothes. I said my father would provide a big house for me. I was thinking my earthly father would do it, but my heavenly father actually already had this place ready for me.

Psalm 27:10 When my father and my mother forsake me, then the Lord will take me up.

John 14:1-3 Let not your heart be troubled: ye believe in God, believe also in me. [2] In my Father's house are many mansions: if it were not so, I would have told you. I go to prepare a place for you. [3] And if I go and prepare a place for you, I will come again, and receive you unto myself; that where I am, there ye may be also.

As a child I was called a mistake, but this is what my God said about it

Genesis 1:26 And God said, Let us make man in our image, after our likeness: and let them have dominion over the fish of the sea, and over the fowl of the air, and over the cattle, and over all the earth, and over every creeping thing that creepeth upon the earth.

Jeremiah 1:5 Before I formed thee in the belly I knew thee; and before thou camest forth out of the womb I sanctified thee, and I ordained thee a prophet unto the nations.

Chapter 2   Teen Years

I was born in sin and therefore made sinful decisions on my own that were setting a pattern for life. I would later live to regret those decisions.

Psalm 51:5 Behold, I was shapen in iniquity; and in sin did my mother conceive me.

Romans 7:17-18 Now then it is no more I that do it, but sin that dwelleth in me. [18] For I know that in me (that is, in my flesh,) dwelleth no good thing: for to will is present with me; but how to perform that which is good I find not.(23) But I see another law in my members, warring against the law of my mind, and bringing me into captivity to the law of sin which is in my members. [24] O wretched man that I am! who shall deliver me from the body of this death? [25] I thank God through Jesus Christ our Lord. So then with the mind I myself serve the law of God; but with the flesh the law of sin.

1 John 1:8-10 If we say that we have no sin, we deceive ourselves, and the truth is not in us. [9] If we confess our sins, he is faithful and just to forgive us our sins, and to cleanse us from all unrighteousness. [10] If we say that we have not sinned, we make him a liar, and his word is not in us.

Chapter 4   Coming to America

I thank God for the foundation of America, for all the men and women that laid down their lives and those still fighting for the freedom that we have. I especially love the freedom to worship the Lord as His Word tells us to. Use your freedom and proclaim the Good News about Jesus.

John 4:21-24 Jesus saith unto her, Woman, believe me, the hour cometh, when ye shall neither in this mountain, nor yet at Jerusalem, worship the Father. [22] Ye worship ye know not what: we know what we worship: for salvation is of the Jews. [23] But the hour cometh, and now is, when the true worshippers shall worship the Father in spirit and in truth: for the Father seeketh such to worship him. [24] God is a Spirit: and they that worship him must worship him in spirit and in truth.

Chapter 5   Getting Out

Many have been deceived to believe that there are no consequences to suicide, yet without knowledge of God. I was worried what might happen to my soul. This fear was inside me, and I did not know how it got there.

Deut. 30:19 I call heaven and earth to record this day against you, that I have set before you life and death, blessing and cursing: therefore choose life, that both thou and thy seed may live:

Proverbs 18:21 Death and life are in the power of the tongue: and they that love it shall eat the fruit thereof.

1 Peter 3:10-11 For he that will love life, and see good days, let him refrain his tongue from evil, and his lips that they speak no guile: [11] Let him eschew evil, and do good; let him seek peace, and ensue it

Romans 2:11-15 For there is no respect of persons with God. [12] For as many as have sinned without law shall also perish without law: and as many as have sinned in the law shall be judged by the law; [13] (For not the hearers of the law are just before God, but the doers of the law shall be justified. [14] For when the Gentiles, which have not the law, do by nature the things contained in the law, these, having not the law, are a law unto themselves: [15] Which shew the work of the law written in their hearts, their conscience also bearing witness, and their thoughts the mean while accusing or else excusing one another;)

Psalm 68:20 He that is our God is the God of salvation; and unto God the Lord belong the issues from death.

Chapter 6   The Vision

Satan is only as big as you allow him to be. His words are powerless unless you believe him. When he speaks, his words fall to the ground going nowhere. When God speaks, the earth trembles as His Word goes out forever, never ending, circling the earth.

Acts 2:17 And it shall come to pass in the last days, saith God,I will pour out of my Spirit upon all flesh: and your sons and your daughters shall prophesy, and your young men shall see visions, and your old men shall dream dreams:

Isaiah 55:11 So shall my word be that goeth forth out of my mouth: it shall not return unto me void, but it shall accomplish that which I please, and it shall prosper in the thing whereto I sent it.

Psalm 34:7 The angel of the Lord encampeth round about them that fear him, and delivereth them.

Isaiah 14:12-18 How art thou fallen from heaven, O Lucifer, son of the morning! how art thou cut down to the ground, which didst weaken the nations! [13] For thou hast said in thine heart, I will ascend into heaven, I will exalt my throne above the stars of God: I will sit also upon the mount of the congregation, in the sides of the north: [14] I will ascend above the heights of the clouds; I will be like the most High. [15] Yet thou shalt be brought down to hell, to the sides of the pit. [16] They that see thee shall narrowly look upon thee, and consider thee, saying, Is this the man that made the earth to tremble, that did shake kingdoms; [17] That made the world as a wilderness, and destroyed the cities thereof; that opened not the house of his prisoners? [18] All the kings of the nations, even all of them, lie in glory, every one in his order.

Ezekiel 28:17-19 Thine heart was lifted up because of thy beauty, thou hast corrupted thy wisdom by reason of thy brightness: I will cast thee to the ground, I will lay thee before kings, that they may behold thee. [18] Thou hast defiled thy sanctuaries by the multitude of thine iniquities, by the iniquity of thy traffick; therefore will I bring forth a fire from the midst of thee, it shall devour thee, and I will bring thee to ashes upon the earth in the sight of all them that behold thee. [19] All they that know thee among the people shall be astonished at thee: thou shalt be a terror, and never shalt thou be any more.

In remembering the bridge, upon crossing the bridge when I looked back it was as ragged as before we crossed over. I believe this is symbolic of the truth that each person must make their own way over hell. They must experience the Truth in Jesus Christ as an individual. You cannot build the bridge for others, they must accept the truth for themselves

John 14:6 Jesus saith unto him, I am the way, the truth, and the life: no man cometh unto the Father, but by me.

John 8:32 And ye shall know the truth, and the truth shall make you free.

Matthew 4:8-11 Again, the devil taketh him up into an exceeding high mountain, and sheweth him all the kingdoms of the world, and the glory of them; [9] And saith unto him, All these things will I give thee, if thou wilt fall down and worship me. [10] Then saith Jesus unto him, Get thee hence, Satan: for it is written, Thou shalt worship the Lord thy God, and him only shalt thou serve. [11] Then the devil leaveth him, and, behold, angels came and ministered unto him.

Ephes. 6:10-12 Finally, my brethren, be strong in the Lord, and in the power of his might. [11] Put on the whole armour of God, that ye may be able to stand against the wiles of the devil. [12] For we wrestle not against flesh and blood, but against principalities, against powers, against the rulers of the darkness of this world, against spiritual wickedness in high places.

Chapter 9   Relief Is Coming

Where we seek relief is very important. If the relief comes from a bad lifestyle it only delays the destruction. If it comes from a drugstore it doesn't offer release, only delay. Our relief must come from God and His Word.

John 4:13-18 Jesus answered and said unto her, Whosoever drinketh of this water shall thirst again: [14] But whosoever drinketh of the water that I shall give him shall never thirst; but the water that I shall give him shall be in him a well of water springing up into everlasting life. [15] The woman saith unto him, Sir, give me this water, that I thirst not, neither come hither to draw. [16] Jesus saith unto her, Go, call thy husband, and come hither. [17] The woman answered and said, I have no husband. Jesus said unto her, Thou hast well said, I have no husband: [18] For thou hast had five husbands; and he whom thou now hast is not thy husband: in that saidst thou truly.

Psalm 107:19-20 Then they cry unto the Lord in their trouble, and he saveth them out of their distresses. [20] He sent his word, and healed them, and delivered them from their destructions.

Chapter 10   My Conversion

Until we are desperate and at the bottom with nowhere else to turn, we don't usually cry out to God in sincerity. To try bargaining with God is not submitting. You cannot bring anything to the bargaining table. I had to offer myself without reservation; willing to follow his direction in my life.

Luke 7:47-48 Wherefore I say unto thee, Her sins, which are many, are forgiven; for she loved much: but to whom little is forgiven, the same loveth little. [48] And he said unto her, Thy sins are forgiven.

2 Cor. 5:17-18 Therefore if any man be in Christ, he is a new creature: old things are passed away; behold, all things are become new. [18] And all things are of God, who hath reconciled us to himself by Jesus Christ, and hath given to us the ministry of reconciliation;

Psalm 116:1-6 I love the Lord, because he hath heard my voice and my supplications. [2] Because he hath inclined his ear unto me, therefore will I call upon him as long as I live. [3] The sorrows of death compassed me, and the pains of hell gat hold upon me: I found trouble and sorrow. [4] Then called I upon the name of the Lord; O Lord, I beseech thee, deliver my soul. [5] Gracious is the Lord, and righteous; yea, our God is merciful. [6] The Lord preserveth the simple: I was brought low, and he helped me.

Psalm 116:12 What shall I render unto the Lord for all his benefits toward me?

2 Cor. 6:2 (For he saith, I have heard thee in a time accepted, and in the day of salvation have I succoured thee: behold, now is the accepted time; behold, now is the day of salvation.)

Romans 8:15-16 For ye have not received the spirit of bondage again to fear; but ye have received the Spirit of adoption, whereby we cry, Abba, Father. [16] The Spirit itself beareth witness with our spirit, that we are the children of God:

Chapter 11   Forgiving Others

In sharing my story, I have been privileged to share with many people who are in church; yet who have not truly forgiven others and therefore are living a defeated life. They may be trying to be a Christian while avoiding the basic foundations. At the start of my walk with God I had no idea how my forgiving others was effecting God's ability to forgive me. It was not easy, but it was necessary. With God's help I truly forgave everyone. You can also forgive others. Today I truly forgive my mother, and pray for her to call on Jesus and be saved as I am.

1 John 1:9 If we confess our sins, he is faithful and just to forgive us our sins, and to cleanse us from all unrighteousness.

Matthew 6:12-15 And forgive us our debts, as we forgive our debtors. [13] And lead us not into temptation, but deliver us from evil: For thine is the kingdom, and the power, and the glory, for ever. Amen. [14] For if ye forgive men their trespasses, your heavenly Father will also forgive you: [15] But if ye forgive not men their trespasses, neither will your Father forgive your trespasses.

Matthew 18:23-35 Therefore is the kingdom of heaven likened unto a certain king, which would take account of his servants. [24] And when he had begun to reckon, one was brought unto him, which owed him ten thousand talents. [25] But forasmuch as he had not to pay, his lord commanded him to be sold, and his wife, and children, and all that he had, and payment to be made. [26] The servant therefore fell down, and worshipped him, saying, Lord, have patience with me, and I will pay thee all. [27] Then the lord of that servant was moved with compassion, and loosed him, and forgave him the debt. [28] But the same servant went out, and found one of his fellowservants, which owed him an hundred pence: and he laid hands on him, and took him by the throat, saying, Pay me that thou owest. [29] And his fellowservant fell down at his feet, and besought him, saying, Have patience with me, and I will pay thee all. [30] And he would not: but went and cast him into prison, till he should pay the debt. [31] So when his fellowservants saw what was done, they were very sorry, and came and told unto their lord all that was done. [32] Then his lord, after that he had called him, said unto him, O thou wicked servant, I forgave thee all that debt, because thou desiredst me: [33] Shouldest not thou also have had compassion on thy fellowservant, even as I had pity on thee? [34] And his lord was wroth, and delivered him to the tormentors, till he should pay all that was due unto him. [35] So likewise shall my heavenly Father do also unto you, if ye from your hearts forgive not every one his brother their trespasses.

When I was dealing with forgiveness, I thought God was mocking me at first. I thought he was just saying he was there and had suffered like me. I did not know he actually did suffer abandonment, rejection, betrayal, beatings, just as I, and even worse.

Isaiah 53:5-8 But he was wounded for our transgressions, he was bruised for our iniquities: the chastisement of our peace was upon him; and with his stripes we are healed. [6] All we like sheep have gone astray; we have turned every one to his own way; and the Lord hath laid on him the iniquity of us all. [7] He was oppressed, and he was afflicted, yet he opened not his mouth: he is brought as a lamb to the slaughter, and as a sheep before her shearers is dumb, so he openeth not his mouth. [8] He was taken from prison and from judgment: and who shall declare his generation? for he was cut off out of the land of the living: for the transgression of my people was he stricken.

Mark 15:34 And at the ninth hour Jesus cried with a loud voice, saying, Eloi, Eloi, lama sabachthani? which is, being interpreted, My God, my God, why hast thou forsaken me?

Mark 14:18-20 And as they sat and did eat, Jesus said, Verily I say unto you, One of you which eateth with me shall betray me. [19] And they began to be sorrowful, and to say unto him one by one, Is it I? and another said, Is it I? [20] And he answered and said unto them, It is one of the twelve, that dippeth with me in the dish.

Mark 14:65 And some began to spit on him, and to cover his face, and to buffet him, and to say unto him, Prophesy: and the servants did strike him with the palms of their hands.

John 19:1-3 Then Pilate therefore took Jesus, and scourged him. [2] And the soldiers platted a crown of thorns, and put it on his head, and they put on him a purple robe, [3] And said, Hail, King of the Jews! and they smote him with their hands.

Chapter 12 A Job from God

Luke 1:49 For he that is mighty hath done to me great things; and holy is his name.

Psalm 91:11 For he shall give his angels charge over thee, to keep thee in all thy ways.

Proverbs 3:6 In all they ways acknowledge him, and he shall direct they paths.

Psalm 37:23 The steps of a good man are ordered by the Lord: and he delighteth in his way.

Matthew 6:33 But seek ye first the kingdom of God, and his righteousness; and all these things shall be added unto you.

Psalm 1:3 And he shall be like a tree planted by the rivers of water, that bringeth forth his fruit in his season; his leaf also shall not wither; and whatsoever he doeth shall prosper.

Exodus 33:19 And he said, I will make all my goodness pass before thee, and I will proclaim the name of the Lord before thee; and will be gracious to whom I will be gracious, and will shew mercy on whom I will shew mercy.

Deut. 28:14 And thou shalt not go aside from any of the words which I command thee this day, to the right hand, or to the left, to go after other gods to serve them.

Psalm 4:1&3 Hear me when I call, O God of my righteousness: thou hast enlarged me when I was in distress; have mercy upon me, and hear my prayer.. [3] But know that the Lord hath set apart him that is godly for himself: the Lord will hear when I call unto him.

Psalm 31:19 Oh how great is thy goodness, which thou hast laid up for them that fear thee; which thou hast wrought for them that trust in thee before the sons of men!

Chapter 15 My husband

When I made choices in relationships it always turned out wrong and destructive. When I let God direct me, it has been peaceful and fulfilling. The oneness that my husband and I share has opened many doors of sharing God's love and peace to others.

Ephes. 5:31 For this cause shall a man leave his father and mother, and shall be joined unto his wife, and they two shall be one flesh.

Psalm 66:19-20 But verily God hath heard me; he hath attended to the voice of my prayer. [20] Blessed be God, which hath not turned away my prayer, nor his mercy from me.

Chapter 17   God Uses My Testimony

My testimony may sound dramatic and quite different, yet I find it is all too common. Many of the women I speak to each day have the same issues hidden back behind their outward shell. I can see through it by the Holy Spirit. When I share my testimony, I share it for God's glory. You have a testimony as well "SHARE IT." Let God use you.

Mark 5:18-20 And when he was come into the ship, he that had been possessed with the devil prayed him that he might be with him. [19] Howbeit Jesus suffered him not, but saith unto him, Go home to thy friends, and tell them how great things the Lord hath done for thee, and hath had compassion on thee. [20] And he departed, and began to publish in Decapolis how great things Jesus had done for him: and all men did marvel.

Jude 1:21-25 Keep yourselves in the love of God, looking for the mercy of our Lord Jesus Christ unto eternal life. [22] And of some have compassion, making a difference: [23] And others save with fear, pulling them out of the fire; hating even the garment spotted by the flesh. [24] Now unto him that is able to keep you from falling, and to present you faultless before the presence of his glory with exceeding joy, [25] To the only wise God our Saviour, be glory and majesty, dominion and power, both now and ever. Amen.

1 John 5:5 Who is he that overcometh the world, but he that believeth that Jesus is the Son of God?

Matthew 4:19-20 And he saith unto them, Follow me, and I will make you fishers of men. [20] And they straightway left their nets, and followed him.

My prayer of thanks:

Dear Lord;

I thank you for choosing me. I thank you for having me in your hands before I was in my mother's womb. Thank you for your grace and mercy in my life. Thank you for forgiving me and setting me free. Thank you for loving me. Thank you for my husband. Thank you for life and my children, grandchildren, and brothers and sisters in Christ. Thank you for my family and all that you have done in my life. Thank you for the call you have on my life to testify for and about you. Until I see you face to face, I love you. Help me to follow you completely each and every day.